MUSTANG
The Original Muscle Car

RANDY LEFFINGWELL

MOTORBOOKS

Dedication

This book is dedicated to the late James G. Coe (1918–1992), my uncle, who bought his early
1965 D-code 289 Guardsman blue, three-speed convertible (with red vinyl interior and white top)
in the summer of 1964 and kept his Mustang for the rest of his life.

This edition published in 2003 by Motorbooks International, an imprint of MBI Publishing Company, Galtier Plaza, Suite 200, 380 Jackson Street, St. Paul, MN 55101-3885 USA

First published in 1995 by MBI Publishing Company.

The information in this book is true and complete to the best of our knowledge. All recommendations are made without any guarantee on the part of the author or Publisher, who also disclaim any liability incurred in connection with the use of this data or specific details.

We recognize that some words, model names and designations, for example, mentioned herein are the property of the trademark holder. We use them for identification purposes only. This is not an official publication.

Motorbooks International titles are also available at discounts in bulk quantity for industrial or sales-promotional use. For details write to Special Sales Manager at Motorbooks International Wholesalers & Distributors, Galtier Plaza, Suite 200, 380 Jackson Street, St. Paul, MN 55101-3885 USA.

ISBN 0-7603-1840-9

Front cover:
The original 1964-1/2 Mustang, together with a 1994 version of Ford's ultimate muscle car. *Mike Mueller*

On the frontispiece:
Three hi-po ponies: The very rare 1968 Shelby GT500KR, a 1965 GT, and a 1994 Cobra.

On the title page:
For 1969 and 1970 Ford pulled out all the stops, offering the fire-breathing Boss 429 crammed ever so tightly beneath the Mustang's hood. Boss indeed.

On the back cover:
Introduced in 1969, the Boss 429 was the biggest, baddest Boss Mustang ever built. *Mike Mueller.*

Cover Design by Koechel Peterson & Associates, Minneapolis, Minnesota

Printed in Hong Kong

Contents

Acknowledgments

My first thanks go to Bob Casey, Curator of Automotive History; to James C. McCabe, Team Leader, Collections Management and Care; and to Luke Gilliland-Swetlund, Team Leader, Access Services; at The Henry Ford Museum & Greenfield Village, Dearborn, Michigan, for their assistance in giving me unrestricted access to Mustang I.

My deep thanks go to Dan Krehbiel, Placentia, California, for his 1946 Sportsman, and to George Watts, Anaheim, California, for his 1955 Thunderbird, the first regular production car, and to Randy Mason, Topanga, California, for his 1956 Lincoln Continental.

The owners of the Mustangs shown within this book patiently put up with my requests for just one more angle, one more move, one more shot. I thank Gary Bergeron, Sacramento, California; Chuck Boughourian, West Hills, California; Peter Bronken, Bozeman, Montana; Chuck Brown, Los Altos, California; David Buracchio, Joshua Tree, California; Otis Chandler, Ojai, California; Judy Cigler, Bozeman, Montana; Lyle Cigler, Bozeman, Montana; Ron Collins, Marion, Indiana; Stephen and Debbie Donovan-Earle, Santa Barbara, California; Kenn and Gil Funk, Glendale, California; Mike Ford, Helena, Montana; Kurt and Cindie Kline, Grand Rapids, Michigan; Dave Kunz, North Hollywood, California; Tony Navarra, San Jose, California; Tom and Carol Podemski, South Bend, Indiana; Doug and Brian Reid, Whittier, California; Buzz Rose, Helena, Montana; John Rosengrant, Glendale, California; Will Rupprecht, Denver, North Carolina; Jerry Sewell, Thousand Oaks, California; Scott Smith, Cupertino, California; Ed Swart, Torrance, California; Paul Vanderheyden, Arroyo Grandé, California; and Dale von Trebra, Santa Paula, California.

Dozens of national and local Ford Mustang owners organizations exist throughout the world to protect and promote information and enthusiasm for the car. A number of these clubs and registries were most helpful. In particular, I thank Gary Bergeron, Sacramento Area Mustang Owner's Club, Sacramento, California; Gary Bettencourt, NorCal chapter Shelby American Automobile Club, Sacramento, California; Rich and Stacie Ciaffredo, San Jose Vintage Mustang Owners Association, California; Larry and Jason Franzen, Sierra Mustang Club, Fair Oaks, California; Vic Hamshar, Sacramento Area Mustang Owner's Club, Sacramento, California; Gary Hansen, T-5 Registry, Livermore, California; David LaRocque, SVO Owners Association, Sudbury, Ontario, Canada; Frank Morales, Orange County Mustang Club, Anaheim, California; and Chris Richardson with the 1965–1969 Mustang GT Registry.

I am most grateful to Jack Roush, founder of Roush Racing and Roush Technologies, Livonia, Michigan, for elaborating on the history of Mustang Pace Cars and his involvement with them at Indianapolis and in the PPG IndyCar series.

I am very grateful also to Bob Perkins, Juneau, Wisconsin, for his time, cooperation, and philosophy. Bob provided not only several extraordinary automobiles but he also taught me what to look for and how to understand what I was seeing.

My sincere thanks also to Ms. Kim Kapin and Jim Yates of A&I Color, Hollywood, California, for their constant critical care and handling of all of my Kodachrome film.

I am immensely indebted to Larry Armstrong, Director of Photography; Terry Schwadron, Assistant Managing Editor; and Shelby Coffey III, Editor, *Los Angeles TIMES* for granting me the leave of absence during which time I worked on this project.

Lastly, the history of the Mustang is the story of the work and accomplishments of thousands of individuals. I want to thank Charles Gumushian, retired Product Launch Manager, North American Public Affairs—and one of those thousands—for his careful examination of the text and his wise and thoughtful suggestions.

Finally, I thank Robert D. Negstad, retired project manager with Ford Motor Company. His experience and wisdom, and his memories, archives, and records, as well as his sense of humor provided not only history but a sense of perspective. Without his generous help, this book would be very much less.

Randy Leffingwell
Los Angeles, California

Introduction
History and Prehistory

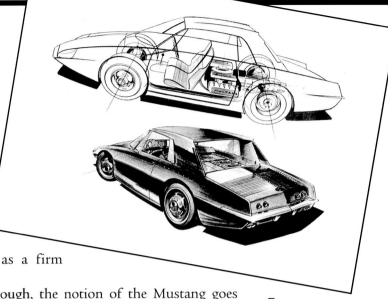

There are those who say the Ford Mustang was born on April 17, 1964, in a large park near New York City in front of an audience of thousands of interested spectators. Earlier that morning, the world had first glimpsed Ford's new car in all the newspapers, on television newscasts, and on the cover of *TIME* and *Newsweek* magazines. Others suggest it was born on October 7, 1962, when a diminutive, mid-engine, rocket-profile, two-seater shot up to 120 miles per hour and ran laps around Watkins Glen International Race Track, igniting a wildfire of enthusiasm that took considerable work to contain. Still others suggest that it was really born about twenty-two weeks before that, on May 8, 1962, when a transplanted engineer from Ford of England, Royston C. Lunn, was assigned to create a car for that Watkins Glen appearance. But those who advocate that date are mostly engineers and designers, people who were intimately involved with the project.

So perhaps the birth of the Mustang was really before that, say, on November 2, 1960, when first-generation-American, engineer-turned-salesman Lee Iacocca was named vice president and general manager of Ford Division of Ford Motor Company. (Or, perhaps, it was a week later on November 8, 1960, when a hatless, handsome John F. Kennedy was elected President of the United States? Eight weeks after the election, he asked recently promoted Ford Motor Company President Robert S. McNamara to be his Secretary of Defense, thus conveniently removing at least one roadblock to the Mustang's future.)

Or what about looking back to sometime in, say, early April 1960. That's about the time the staff of *Sports Car Graphic* would have been putting to bed their May/June issue. Art Director Dick Fischer and Editor Warren A. Woron had decided to devote two pages to a feature called "Meet The Mustang." This consisted of drawings of a two-seat, mid-engined, Corvair-powered, steel-bodied, removable-hardtop coupe. It looked something like the later Fiat X1/9. It was incredibly advanced, and it was designed by a trio of former General Motors stylists living in Los Angeles and working together as a firm called IDEA.

Likely, though, the notion of the Mustang goes back further, at least to October 22, 1954. That was the introduction of Ford's two-seat sporting car, the Thunderbird. Back farther still? One or two historians outline the farthest limits of their perspective on the Ford Mustang with the 1946 Ford Sportsman, a postwar, five-passenger convertible with a partially wooden body. It was an almost luxurious signal to Ford buyers that the War was over.

Eighteen years—1946 to 1964—is a long gestation period, even in the context of American automobile design, development, and production. But the discussion here is about the genesis of an automobile that defined an era, not one that merely contributed to the genre. The decade of muscle cars is still today known as the age of the "pony cars." Even though competitors had introduced cars earlier, the period was not called the era of the predator fish, nor of the birds of prey, nor of the . . . well, how does one describe the pony cars from Chevrolet? Corvette, of course, comes from nautical history, and it is generally defined as a fast warship, primarily used as part of a convoy. But from what dictionary came Camaro? Or Corvair? In *Roget's Thesaurus*, they would be most likely found listed under "pony cars."

So perhaps a brief history is in order here, just to bring the context back to April 17, 1964, the official birth date of the Mustang.

Former GM stylists Pete Brock, Gene Garfinkle and Norm Neuman collaborated with engineer Don Nichols to form a company in California called Industrial Design Engineering Associates (IDEA). One of their self-assigned ideas was a styling exercise they called Mustang. They specified a Corvair engine but mounted it midships on a 90-inch wheelbase. They planned for the roof to be removable. Fitted luggage was to be optional and the target price was $4,500. *Courtesy Len Frank Archives*

1

The First Fourteen Years
1946–1960

For Ford, General Motors, and Chrysler, much of the six years of World War II was spent producing materiel for U.S. GIs and American allies. Automobile manufacture effectively stopped in 1941. Design and styling departments were too preoccupied making working drawings of bomb sights, tank track rollers, destroyer hatches, and aircraft engines even to toy around with concepts for possible postwar automobiles.

When the conflict ended in 1945, many soldiers with war-time pay in their pockets came home to wives who'd taken over their industrial jobs and built bombers and savings accounts. A half-decade of denial of material possessions created a large demand for new automobiles. Studebaker and Hudson, both independent and less occupied with materiel production during the war, quickly introduced brand new models. But the Big Three were forced to dust off 1941 tooling and reintroduce familiar products.

In 1946, there was a small demand for something nicer than the run-of-the-mill, re-labeled 1941 models. Ford—as well as Chrysler and Nash—introduced runs of limited-production wood-trimmed cars. These were evocative of the rich custom-body era of the 1930s. The car makers used mahogany veneer framed with white ash, yellow birch, or maple. These were a kind of mass-produced personal-luxury car. Chrysler's Town & Country convertibles and sedans sold 12,000 copies by 1951. Nash's Suburban sold barely 1,000, but it caught viewers' attention and brought them in to dealerships to look at other models. Ford and Mercury Divisions each produced a Sportsman model—some 3,500 from Ford (but only 205 from Mercury). These, too, were very good for showroom traffic. But more importantly, they suggested to Ford management that the marketplace was interested in a stylish, personal automobile.

In 1949, each of the Big Three—as well as the independents—introduced new models. Chrome and two-tone paint replaced the wood. The idea of exclusive, factory-special cars, not only from the premium divisions such as Cadillac and Lincoln, but from Ford and Chevrolet , had become part of the foundation of the postwar car business.

In the early 1950s, Max Hoffman, a Viennese automobile enthusiast, opened a showroom on Fifth Avenue in New York City and began to fill it with cars from Germany and England. Mercedes-Benz sedans—but also 190SL sports cars—and Jaguar XK120 sports cars—but also sedans—vied for floor space with Triumph TR2s, Austin-Healey 100s, Alfa Romeo Giulias, and Porsche 356s. Hoffman was offering the same sports cars that returning GIs—taken with their road-holding, liveliness, and economy—had brought home from abroad. These cars had individual bucket-type seats and manual four-speed transmissions with floor-mounted shift levers.

For Ford, Chrysler, and General Motors, the floor shift was too much like the Model A and other early cars. The Big Three had done that before, and America was too prosperous after the war to do it again. Americans could afford a machine to do the shifting for them. What's more, sports car sales in the U.S. were nearly inconsequential.

Italian designer Pinin Farina and Englishman Donald Healey introduced a Nash-engined two-seater in 1951. Called the Nash-Healey, pro-

Above and opposite
1946 Ford Sportsman
Ford Styling Director Bob Gregorie wrapped the back end of a Model A in white ash, yellow birch, and mahogany to produce a custom-body appearance at an affordable price. Henry Ford II liked the idea and authorized limited production. Sales amounted to about 3,500 from 1946 through 1948. A Mercury version was offered only in 1946, and only 205 sold. Both were powered by Ford's 100 horsepower flat-head V-8.

duction was set at 200 per year. Its sales (and its performance) were slow, and so Americans took little notice when designer Howard "Dutch" Darrin collaborated with Henry Kaiser to build a fiberglass-bodied two-seater on the chassis of the Henry J, Kaiser's economy model. Called the Kaiser-Darrin, it was introduced in 1953. Only 437 Kaiser-Darrins were built. Predictably, America barely noticed when 300 copies of a new, all-fiberglass two-seater rolled off a Chevrolet production line later that same year.

Chevrolet took a big gamble when it put its Blue Flame Six in front of its two-speed automatic transmission and surrounded it with a product named after the U.S. and English Navy's convoy escorts, the corvettes. It quickened the pulse of some car shoppers, but for those more enamored of Cadillac Eldorados with polished fins, it hastened their retreat from Chevrolet show rooms. No matter. Enough of them sold in 1954 (3,540) that Chevrolet stuck with it, and Ford was convinced to offer its own two-seater sporty.

Henry Ford II was called home from the Navy during the war to run the company that his father was by then too ill to manage. He reacted quickly to all the problems facing the business. His solutions worked well, and by the early 1950s, Ford Motor Company had settled firmly into second place behind General Motors. If Chevrolet had a Corvette, Ford would make a better one. The Corvette had plastic side curtains like the British MGs and Triumphs; Ford's two-seater would have proper roll-up windows. Chevrolet had a six-cylinder engine, Ford would have a V-8. Henry wanted it that way, and Ford Division's vice president and general manager, Lewis D. Crusoe, would see that it got done.

When the 1955 Thunderbird was introduced on October 22, 1954, it offered all of these features and more. Even though Chevrolet had upgraded its Corvette to V-8 power, it was obvious to anyone taking notes that Ford had guessed right. The Thunderbird's lines, designed by Robert Maguire and Damon Woods, were clean and simple, adorned only with rudimentary fins. While Chevrolet sold 675 of its 1955 Corvettes, Ford sold 16,155 of its Thunderbirds. Although Thunderbird sales for 1956 slipped about 5 percent, new tail fins, a new interior, and redesigned front bumpers and grille boosted 1957 sales to 21,380.

Crusoe was less of an automobile enthusiast than he was an observer of customers' natures. A story reported in Gary Witzenburg's book, *Mustang*, is evidence of the way that many of Ford's general managers have had of sniffing the air and recognizing the trends.

"A few weeks," Witzenburg wrote, "before the 1955 Thunderbird was presented to the public—as product planner Tom Case remembers—Lew Crusoe, then Ford Division general manager, drove one home to see how it checked out on the road. Following a weekend with the new car, Crusoe called Case into his office on Monday morning.

"'Tom,' he said, 'there is one thing wrong with the Thunderbird. It's a beautiful car, but we need a rear seat in it. Let's go to work and make a four-passenger 'Bird.'"

The car grew, but in ways not exactly anticipated. What had begun life as a somewhat luxurious sporting car could not slip back into mundane business-coupe status. Leg room, head room, and comfortable seating for rear passengers were needed, as well as a trunk large enough for all of their baggage. By the 1958 introduction, the car had gained about 430 pounds. Performance that had been very robust with two seats in 1957 would not be permitted to diminish with four. But Ford had not yet fully developed its thin-wall V-8 engine technology. In 1958, big power still meant big engines with big weight. The 300 horsepower that was optional for 1957 was the standard for '58.

Crusoe was right. Even with a mid-year introduction, something like 40,000 cars were sold. This figure more than doubled by the end of 1960. Across America, buyers wanted to be able to take with them their children or their friends or their golf bags and still travel in style. Crusoe described the new four-seater on the day of its introduction. It had become, as Allan Nevins and Frank Hill quoted in their 1963 book, *Ford: Decline And Rebirth*, "more truly a personal or boulevard car for the customer who insists on comfort and yet would like to own a prestige vehicle that incorporates the flair and performance characteristics of a sports car." As the Thunderbird

swerved farther away from the route that the Corvette had followed, it evolved into a luxury car even as the purists wailed over Ford's road not taken.

At any of the automakers, sharp decisions that produce large sales increases—especially increases that bring new customers to Ford rather than just shifting alliances within the product line—are rewarded with promotion. For Crusoe, his move came along as he contemplated the bigger Bird. On January 25, 1955, he became executive vice president, Car and Truck Division, making him responsible for assembly and distribution of all Ford vehicles. Soon after, he also was named chairman of the Product Planning Committee.

Robert S. McNamara, a Californian who had joined Ford in 1946 after service in the Air Force, had been a Harvard business school professor before the war. He had been one of the ten officers who ran the Air Force Office of Statistical Control. His familiarity with accounting, cost control, and marketing led him to work with Crusoe on Ford corporate financial matters. However, he was decidedly not a car buff.

McNamara's philosophy was basically that Ford Division should not produce any automobile that didn't sell in numbers large enough to make a profit. Yet Henry Ford II and Lew Crusoe

1955 Ford Thunderbird
The two-seat American sports car era began in 1951 with the Nash-Healey. By 1953, Chevrolet had its fiberglass-bodied Corvette and Henry Kaiser had collaborated with body designer Howard "Dutch" Darrin to produce another fiberglass two-seater, the Kaiser-Darrin. Each of these was powered by an in-line six-cylinder engine until Chevrolet introduced its 256 cubic-inch V-8 in 1955, the same year Ford brought out its Thunderbird with a 292-cubic-inch V-8.

Lewis Crusoe was Ford Division general manager and his idea was to beat General Motors at its own product game. From the start, Ford's T-Bird had roll-up windows unlike the first Corvettes which had British sports-car-like side curtains. Ford delivered the car for $2,944, and it outsold Chevrolet's two-seater by more than twenty to one. Still, Crusoe believed from the first that the car needed four seats.

both liked the Thunderbird; McNamara supported the redesign to four seats.

While the question of the sports car market was answered with Ford's personal luxury car, a new, different market was struggling for recognition. Ford—and GM and Chrysler—could not fail to notice the inroads made by Volkswagen and Renault on American highways. Ford reacted as it had done with the Corvette: quickly and strongly. It introduced the Falcon in 1959 and sold an astonishing 417,174 cars in its first twelve months. For the same season, Chrysler introduced its Valiant, and Chevrolet brought out its air-cooled, rear-engine Corvair. None of these three was a show stopper visually, but, certainly in the case of the Falcon, it was not for lack of effort. A number

of drawings had conceived the Falcon differently. Roof lines and fenders had a variety of other shapes before the final design was approved.

However, Bob McNamara, part of the Ford management group admiringly known as the Whiz Kids, had no interest in questioning design decisions. This was especially true when the sales volume of the car that matched his pragmatic, profit-oriented plans had set so high a record. But there were others who asked themselves, how many more cars might have sold if . . . ?

One individual for whom those questions would become relevant was Lee Iacocca. He already had made his mark selling Fords in Pennsylvania. He earned his undergraduate degree from Lehigh University and a masters from Princeton, both in mechanical engineering. He had known from the time he was fourteen that he wanted to work at Ford—he owned a 1938 flathead while at Lehigh—and in 1946 he joined the company as a student engineer. But after nine months of his eighteen-month introduction program at the huge River Rouge plant in Dearborn, he was bored and disillusioned. Years later he wrote about it in his 1984 book, *Lee Iacocca: An Autobiography*. After spending an entire day making a detailed drawing of a clutch spring, he wondered, "Is this how I want to be spending the rest of my life?

"I wanted to stay at Ford," Iacocca wrote, "but not in engineering. I was eager to be where the real action was—marketing or sales. I liked working with people more than machines." But Ford would not transfer him to sales so he quit. A short time later, he rejoined Ford Motor Company, working for Eastern Division Sales Manager Charles Beacham.

By 1956, when he was only thirty-two, Iacocca had caught Robert McNamara's attention. Iacocca had invented a sales promotion: "20% down and $56 a month for a '56 Ford." McNamara, thirty-nine, Ford Division vice president and general manager since January 1955, instituted the promotion nationwide and later assessed that Iacocca's "$56 for '56" idea contributed to an additional 72,000 car sales that year. It earned the innovative engineer-turned salesman an invitation back to Dearborn, and a ride in the fast lane up into Ford management.

McNamara's unexciting Falcon continued to roll out of the factory doors at a fast pace. But by 1960 Chevrolet had upped the ante, improving the image of its staid Corvair by introducing the Monza, a performance-oriented option package. The bench seat was replaced with two buckets, the two-speed automatic that shifted on the dash was supplanted by a four-speed on the floor, the dashboard got more instruments, and the floors got carpeting. The Falcon, a symbol of McNamara's fondness for frugal, utilitarian transport, looked like a pale cousin at the beach on a sunny day.

Still, Ford Motor Company rewarded sales volume with promotion. On Wednesday, November 9, 1960, Robert S. McNamara was elected president of Ford Motor Company by its board of directors. A cautious, financial manager who was both an intellectual and a Democrat, he voted the day before, Tuesday, November 8, for another intellectual Democrat, and by the time of McNamara's announcement, Republican candidate Richard Nixon had conceded, and the United States had elected a new president as well. Within a month, President-elect John F. Kennedy had offered Ford Motor Company's President-elect a chance to manage the military he had once served. McNamara accepted the cabinet post as Secretary of Defense on December 13.

A week before McNamara's and Kennedy's new appointments, Iacocca was promoted to fill the job McNamara had vacated five years earlier—vice president and general manager, Ford Division. For Lee Iacocca, a man who had set goals for himself throughout his life, he had achieved his ambition at age thirty-six, just about a year behind his target date.

McNamara left quickly, sacrificing a $410,000 salary for $25,000 and civil service. Iacocca suddenly felt an unexpected burden. While his performance had been excellent, he knew that he lacked what all his predecessors had accomplished. "I had no real credentials as a product man," he wrote. "At this point in my career there was no car that people could point to and say: 'Iacocca did that one.'"

1956 Lincoln Continental Mark II
It was the ultimate Ford product. Introduced in 1956, the Lincoln Continental Mark II sold for $10,000, more than a Ferrari sports car and nearly as much as a Rolls-Royce sedan. Bob Gregorie's elegant body didn't roll down the newly established Interstate Highways so much as it hovered over them, elegant, aloof, exclusive. The styling reflected the custom-designed body era of the 1930s common to Rolls-Royce, Packard, and Duesenberg. Its long hood emphasized its power; its short rear deck emphasized the idea that this car was not meant to carry goods—or even baggage—only people. Even at $10,000 each, Ford lost money on every one. Style and prestige have always been costly.

2

Speeding 120 Miles Per Hour in the Wrong Direction
November 1960–October 1962

Lee Iacocca admired Bob McNamara. The Harvard professor had taught the Princeton engineer several valuable lessons. As Iacocca recalled, for any question or in any situation, McNamara knew all the facts. But he also put his lightning-fast mind to work thinking ahead, sorting out the hypothetical considerations as well. McNamara liked multiple answers, plural possibilities, and he always examined all the conceivable causes and effects. But he understood that his subordinates didn't always study things so thoroughly. "Go home tonight," he once told Iacocca, "and put your great idea on paper. If you can't do that, then you haven't really thought it out."

Iacocca did. Since then he has had his subordinates do this kind of homework as well. But he continued to practice what he preached, keeping notes in a small black book he carried with him. One note referred to a roof line sketch for McNamara's Falcon; it had been rejected as impractical. It resembled the early T-bird roof, it had visual appeal, and Iacocca liked it. It led to one of those instances when, despite record first-year sales of the Falcon, Iacocca wondered how many more might have sold if the practical car also had been more stylish and attractive?

Another note examined the identity of Ford Motor Company. General Motors trumpeted its lavish styling under the influence of design chief Bill Mitchell. GM also promoted something it called its "general excellence." Chrysler boasted about its engineering. It had already introduced the Valiant with its in-line "slant-6," and its hemispherical-head, high-performance V-8 engines for the Chrysler 300-series were almost legendary.

But what was Ford? Where was Ford? The 1950s had brought luxury to Ford's image, and now 1960 saw basic transportation reintroduced to the Ford family. McNamara's utilitarian attitude about his Falcon was so strong that some people wondered if he'd secretly wanted the car available only in Ford Model T black.

But McNamara was gone, and Iacocca was in charge of Ford Division now. Henry Ford II himself gave Iacocca a strong shove to follow the same instincts that had gotten him into the division general manager's job in the first place. One of Iacocca's first moves was to gather together eight creative department heads to look at the present and future of Ford Division. The group met after regular working hours—away from the office phones, countless meetings, and daily crises—at Dearborn's new Fairlane Inn less than a mile from World Headquarters. Iacocca chaired this committee.

Around the table each week sat Don Frey, product planning manager, and his special projects assistant Hal Sperlich. Market Research Manager Bob Eggert was there, with Public Relations Manager Walter Murphy as well as Marketing Manager Chase Morsey, Advertising Manager John Bowers, and Sid Olson from J. Walter Thompson, Ford's advertising agency. The eighth member of the Fairlane Committee, as it became known, was Special Projects Manager Jacque Passino. Passino was in effect Ford's racing director.

The agendas for these dinners came from Iacocca's notebooks. The staid appearance of their economy car concerned him. The performance

The welded tubular steel space frame was constructed from 1.0-inch-outer-diameter tube. Front suspension used traditional upper and lower A-arms with coil-over shock absorbers and an anti-sway bar on a 48-inch tread width. The independent rear suspension used an upper A-arm and with a lower inverted A-arm, similar shocks and anti-sway bar on a 49-inch tread width. A four-speed transaxle was fitted with a final drive ratio of 3.30:1.

Opposite
1962 Mustang I
On May 8, 1962, Roy Lunn and a small group of Ford engineers working in research were authorized to build a "show car" to promote the concept of "Total Performance—Powered by Ford." Lunn and his crew were to have it completed, ready for introduction on October 7, a scant twenty-two weeks later— 100 business days, not counting weekends or holidays. For the last six weeks, most of the crew grabbed what sleep they could in the shops.

By early 1962, Lee Iacocca had advanced the idea that Ford should have a sporty car. Head of Styling Gene Bordinat parceled out assignments to consider shapes for the car. John Najjar and Jim Sipple were asked to work on two-seater ideas. Their result looked promising enough on paper to go ahead with a full-size model first in clay. Najjar, an aviation buff, named it Mustang to honor the World War II fighter plane.

advantage that Chevrolet had seized when it introduced the Monza version of its economy Corvair worried him. Ford had no performance options committed for the Falcon. And the weekly mail that Ford received begging for a new, two-passenger Thunderbird alerted him to the growing interest among consumers in their cars' appearance and performance.

"Perhaps," Iacocca mused in his autobiography, "the two-passenger Thunderbird was just ahead of its time . . ."

Chase Morsey and Bob Eggert, with help from marketing's Frank Zimmerman, produced reams of paper that supported the theory that the make-up of America's population was changing. The postwar baby boom had yielded a population that was getting close to career-

starting/car-buying age. Children would soon out-number parents, and there would be more fifteen-to-twenty-nine-year-olds than there would be thirty-to-thirty-nine-year-olds. Annual incomes would exceed $10,000 in three times as many households from 1960 to 1970. Surveys revealed consumer preferences for bucket seats; floor-shifted, four-speed manual transmissions; and an end to fins.

Two other concerns cropped up in Iacocca's black book. Both, unfortunately, bore the imprimatur of his former mentor, Bob McNamara. In view of marketing's survey results, the Falcon was stodgy. Worse, Iacocca knew that a small-car project that McNamara had husbanded through Ford of Germany, a new automobile code-named "Cardinal," was even smaller and less interesting.

Iacocca went home and worked out on paper all the reasons that the Cardinal should be canceled. He would have to sell his decision to Henry Ford II, the man who had authorized $36 million to develop the car. The Cardinal was to be fitted with either an in-line four-cylinder engine from Ford of England or a new V-4 designed and manufactured in Germany (derived from a series of modular engines including the V-4, a V-6 and, in the U.S., a V-8). However, the styling of the boxy little coupes and sedans made the Falcon seem striking by comparison. The Cardinal was configured with front-wheel drive, which allowed for better use of space within the package. But the package held little appeal to a nation that was becoming turned on by rock-and-roll music, tuned up by 300 horsepower V-8s, and transfixed by a new, young president with a stylish wife and two noble-born children.

Iacocca's homework paid off. Ford swallowed the loss on the Cardinal, relegating it to European-only distribution. (As the Taunus, it went on to be very successful, selling millions of cars in the next decade in Europe. But Europe was not America.) For Iacocca, this cancellation signified Ford's acceptance and approval of his vision of the future. And a mandate to make it work.

"The Lively Ones" was the term and the theme that came out of fourteen dinners at the Fairlane Inn. It gave birth to a rapid re-invention of the Falcon for the 1962 model year. A convertible would appear and so would a vinyl-roof/four-on-the-floor Falcon Futura. Similar options would be offered for the recently introduced Fairlane and for the larger Galaxy models as well. The best news for the Falcon was the development of the new 221 cubic-inch V-8, a thin-wall engine that offered much higher horsepower per pound than did the previous high-performance V-8s. Falcons with the 221s were called Sprints.

The "Lively Ones" rapidly evolved into the "Total Performance" theme. This was a three-pronged thrust aimed primarily at General Motors and Chrysler. The performance orientation that these two competitors had pursued in the late 1950s had left Ford behind. Part of this was due to the cautious McNamara, but as much of the responsibility rested with image-conscious Henry Ford II. In June 1957, the Automobile

Manufacturers Association (AMA) had prohibited carmaker's direct participation in racing and any advertising or promotion that emphasized performance. Henry Ford II, whose marketing efforts through the early 1950s had been quality and safety, could not see a way through the conflict that was apparent in these two divergent philosophies. He accepted the ban, and McNamara embraced it.

Performance enthusiasts within Ford smelled a rat and quickly recognized that the AMA ban was being largely ignored by Chevrolet, Pontiac, and Chrysler which continued to support National Association for Stock Car Auto Racing (NASCAR) and United States Auto Club (USAC) efforts rather blatantly via their back doors. Jacque Passino struggled to do what he could to assist long-time Ford racers Holman and Moody and the Wood brothers. But everything done needed to be done cautiously. Henry Ford II could not be made to appear as though he was speaking out of both sides of his mouth.

So Chevrolet and Pontiac laid waste to the NASCAR super ovals and Chrysler took home the trophies from the drag strips. In Europe, Jaguar, Aston-Martin, and Ferrari took endurance race, hill climb, and rally wins, plus headlines. Ford simply was nowhere.

Packed full of innovations adopted from European racing cars, the two-seater had immobile bucket seats whose frame actually aided chassis stiffness. To accommodate a variety of drivers, both the steering column and foot pedals moved forward or back a total of 4 inches. Steering was quick, using a 15.0:1 ratio, with 2.9 turns lock-to-lock. Instrumentation was complete and stylish.

When John Najjar and Jim Sipple looked at engine possibilities, Ford's compact German V-4 fit perfectly into a midship configuration. It kept the cowl and fender line low and encouraged the bullet shape that was soon developed. The body, made of welded aluminum hand hammered into shape by Troutman & Barnes and California Metal Finishers in southern California, surrounded a tubular steel space frame, and both elements together contributed to the car's rigidity.

After loyal palace guardian Bob McNamara left for Camelot, Iacocca went to see Ford. Henry listened as Iacocca described the other companies' back-door racing practices, waited a while, and then continued to watch a little longer. Then he approached General Motors. GM's top management expressed its apologies and its dismay that it was unable to control its division managers who chose to race anyway. Ford didn't want to be the first car maker to openly breach the AMA edict, but GM's answer to him didn't wash. He wrote to the AMA in mid-June 1962. His letter was quoted in Witzenburg's book *Mustang*. "Ford Motor Company feels that the resolution has come to have neither purpose nor effect," Ford wrote in part. "Accordingly, we have notified the board of directors of the Automobile Manufacturers Association that we feel we can better establish our own standards of conduct with respect to the manner in which the performance of our vehicles is to be promoted and advertised."

The gloves were off. Ford was back. The Fairlane Committee had already mapped out its strategy. First up was an official return to racing, initially in NASCAR and then in drag racing at National Hot Rod Association (NHRA) venues. Next was to go after USAC's prestigious Indianapolis 500. In addition, Ford would support sports car racing. And, at the J. Walter Thompson

ad agency's suggestion, Ford would take McNamara's staid Falcon to Europe to compete in the 1963 Monte Carlo Rally. Ford's engines would become the stars; "powered by Ford" would come to mean something.

The second thrust of the "Total Performance" philosophy would take the consumer interest in the two-seat Thunderbird, blend that with the solemn Falcon, and try to make something out of it. Iacocca went to see Ford's styling chief, Gene Bordinat, to compare notes and to discuss possibilities. Bordinat had a surprise for his visitor. Bob Maguire, co-designer of the 1955 Thunderbird, was now head of advanced styling. He had come up with a concept for a smart, stylish four-passenger coupe. The full-size clay model had taken some inspiration from the Thunderbird's long nose and the long-nose/short-tail configuration of Lincoln division's sleek 1956 Continental Mark II. The car, code-named the Allegro, followed those lines; its bucket seats, straddling the transmission tunnel, allowed Maguire to draw an even lower roof line than the Continental.

Iacocca liked it—the idea more than the car itself—and he encouraged Bordinat to explore the possibilities: four seats, two seats and two-plus-two seating where rear leg room might be less than a sedan or standard coupe. These were each configurations that he suggested that Bordinat study.

Iacocca later went to see Tom Case who had become the Falcon planning manager. Iacocca asked Case to thoroughly investigate the factors involved in producing a new four-place car. Case recalled that Budd Company had produced the bodies for the original Thunderbird. As a variation on the research for Iacocca—and with an interest in keeping costs down by using existing body stampings—he wondered if Budd could revise and update the car for new production. Budd got very excited and even produced a prototype. They removed the fins and headlight eyebrows from the '57 Thunderbird body and mounted it onto a modified Falcon chassis. Called the XT-Bird, its proportions never looked quite right, and the costs to produce it seemed too high for the sales it might generate. Furthermore, Iacocca was not sold on the two-seater idea, and so the proposal was abandoned.

Now it was early 1962, and Tom Case had been promoted to manager of special vehicles for Ford and Lincoln-Mercury. Case's study went to product planning manager Don Frey and Hal Sperlich, his special assistant. They were assigned to create a car that would be code-named the "Special Falcon," a sporty car built to a price ($2,500) and a weight (2,500 pounds). Bordinat's group was working on several styling ideas.

Things were beginning to cook at Ford. Department heads were getting excited. "Total Performance" was becoming total involvement. "Powered by Ford" had meant something significant in the Model T days of banked board track racing. Then it had weight in the late 1930s and early 1940s with the legendary flat-head V-8s. It was about to mean something again.

But how could Iacocca let the consumer know?

Outside Ford Motor Company, serendipity and coincidence were waiting in the pits. The concept of "Total Performance—Powered By Ford" was the same as a five-minute warning to "start your engines."

A tall, lanky Texan, Carroll Shelby, wanted to put an American V-8 into a lightweight European sports car. Shelby had won countless races including the 24 Hours of Le Mans in 1959, driving an Aston-Martin. Now retired because of a heart condition, he wanted to build high-performance cars for others to race on the tracks and for consumers to drive on the roads. General Motors turned down his proposal; it wasn't willing to compromise its Corvette or to put it at risk. So in August 1961, Shelby came to Ford with the hope of acquiring some of the new 260 cubic-inch V-8s. Racing manager Jacque Passino liked Shelby's idea and saw in him a testing and development arrangement that, if successful, would further the concept of "Powered by Ford." He approved the sale and shipment of some engines, and Shelby went to work. His first prototype ran on January 30, 1962, in England at Silverstone Racing Circuit.

But the question nagged—how to let the consumer know what was going on *inside* Ford? How to tell them that things at the Blue Oval were changing. In late spring, even while Shelby's Cobra had gotten lots of magazine attention after its tests at the end of January, it was still called

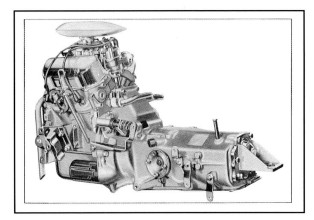

the Shelby Cobra. It started the sizzle, but it was not quite the big steak Ford hoped to fry.

Then in July 1962, a month after Henry Ford II's AMA letter, and as Shelby was beginning production of his Cobra for racing and street sales, Dan Gurney, a former Porsche Formula One driver from California, arrived in Dearborn with English car builder Colin Chapman. They had an idea of their own. In 1961, Jack Brabham had raced a four-cylinder rear-engined Cooper-Climax at Indy, failing to finish. In May 1962, Gurney had driven a rear-engine Buick V-8-powered car for Mickey Thompson that also failed to finish. Engine durability was always the culprit. Gurney and Chapman needed, they said, a reliable 350 horsepower from a lightweight engine. Their timing was as sharp as Shelby's had been. Don

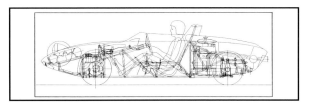

Frey and Dave Evans had watched Gurney in Thompson's car during the race and had come to similar conclusions. Driving back north to Dearborn from Indianapolis, they had begun to plan what it would take to build an Indy-winning engine. A deal was done. Chapman's Lotus would be "Powered by Ford."

By the time Gurney and Chapman visited Passino, the third element of the "Total Performance" program had already gotten under way. It had occurred in a small meeting held on May 8

Left and below
The 60-degree V-4 engine was to be offered in two states of tune for the Mustang. For the street, the 1,500-cubic-centimeter engine was to produced 89 horsepower at 6,600 rpm and 89 foot-pounds of torque at 3,600 rpm while a racing tune would produce 109 horsepower at 6,400 rpm and 99 foot-pounds torque. It was a very simple overhead-valve design, originally destined for Robert McNamara's pet economy car project, the Cardinal. *Kerry Morse archives*

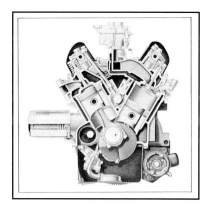

Roy Lunn presented a paper prepared by Charlie Maddox and Norm Postma to the Society of Automotive Engineers (SAE). Typically, SAE papers are chock full of illustrations, charts, and photographs to demonstrate and explain the engineering developments of significance that were accomplished. This package drawing shows placement of key features. *Bob Negstad archives*

even before the 500-mile race. It had been just another coincidence waiting to happen. Ford Motor Company Engineering Vice President Herb Misch knew what cars the corporation would bring out in the fall for the 1963 model year. They were the first of a series of more appealing automobiles. He and Cog Briggs, the public relations liaison for his department, concluded that a concept vehicle—something that would stop auto show visitors and journalists in their tracks—would be a way to promote the new line-up. As a show car, it didn't need to run, just to look sensational.

Earlier in the year, when Iacocca had visited Bordinat with the goal of generating some new sporty-car designs, one of the ideas that surfaced was a mid-engined two-seater. Bordinat assigned

1955 Thunderbird stylists Bob Maguire and Damon Woods to oversee all the projects. They, in turn, assigned executive stylists John Najjar and Jim Sipple to work on a couple of two-seater ideas.

Some time before this, Frank Theyleg, the drivetrain engineer who had supervised development of the McNamara economy Cardinal with its front-wheel-drive V-4 engine, had become

Left
The engine was a 60-degree V-4 with bore and stroke of 3.54x2.32 inches for 91.4-cubic-inch displacement, almost exactly 1500 cubic centimeters. Two versions were planned, a street version producing 89 horsepower at 6,600 rpm with 89 foot-pounds of torque at 3,600 rpm and a racing model with 109 horsepower at 6,400 rpm and 99 foot-pounds of torque at 5,200 rpm. Compression ratio for either model was quoted as 11.0:1.

Opposite
Najjar and Sipple incorporated a roll bar into the design and styling of the Mustang. While Lunn's bosses only specified a show car, he and his crew meant from the start to provide a fully functional automobile built to current Sports Car Club of America regulations. The exhaust pipes protruded through the body, a feature that would reappear on production GTs beginning in April 1965.

Lower left
The manufacturer's data plate records its serial number, 1M1500, signifying its unique status and engine displacement. The dual-brake-system reservoirs and the clutch fluid reservoir are mounted in a movable framework, adjustable a total of 4 inches for driver's leg length. The battery fit in a tray between the reservoirs and number plate, mounted in front for better weight distribution.

Much of the experience and learning from this car was passed on, but not into production. Lunn and many of his crew went to England to work on Ford's GT40s. This Mustang stood 39.4 inches tall to the top of the roll bar. Built on a 90-inch wheelbase, it was 154.3 inches long overall, 61 inches wide, and weighed only 1,544 pounds with 13 gallons of gas in the tank. (This was 10 inches shorter, 9 inches narrower, and 1 inch lower than the GT40.) Weight distribution was 46.85 percent front, 53.2 percent rear. Only two were built, this running model and a second "push-around" display version.

friends with another front-wheel-drive advocate, Roy Lunn, an English chassis engineer who had been transplanted from Ford of England. Theyleg and Lunn were both sports-car enthusiasts, and they wondered if the Cardinal V-4 with its transaxle could be adapted for use in a mid-engined, lightweight sports car.

When the Cardinal was killed, "Total Performance" took over Ford Division attention. Theyleg and Lunn understood that, at least for the time being, "Powered By Ford" signified eight-cylinder vee engines, not fours.

But that was only until Herb Misch and Cog Briggs saw a Najjar/Sipple design for a small, mid-engined sports car that they could use for their show-car purposes. Misch authorized it, and on May 8, Roy Lunn, who was an executive engineer in research by that time, was assigned to make it work. After all, "Powered By Ford" did not mean "pushed around by Ford employees." Lunn picked his own crew to accomplish the feat. And feat it would be: Misch wanted the car ready to introduce to journalists and consumers at the October 7, 1962, United States Grand Prix in Watkins Glen, New York. That was only twenty-two weeks away, 100 days not counting weekends or the Memorial Day, Independence Day, and Labor Day holidays.

A fresh-scrubbed, young engineer from Oregon State University, Bob Negstad, had been hired in 1956. Working in the same college graduate training program that Lee Iacocca had experienced, he became fascinated by front-wheel-drive technology and began investigating its chassis, steering geometry, and suspensions in the drafting room on his own time after his regular hours. He read, studied, and drew, and studied some more. About a year and a half into his two-year program, his enterprise was noticed, and he was made a full engineer and transferred to work on the German Cardinal front-wheel-drive project.

Other work in Europe and England rounded out Negstad's education and skills, and he returned to the U.S. in time to participate in Herb Misch's show-car project. Lunn tagged Negstad to be his assistant to handle chassis development while working with other engineers including Norm Postma, Charlie Maddox, Len Bailey, Chuck Mountain, Bud Anderson, and designer Jim Graham.

On May 9, they began with Najjar's drawings, and all of them quickly concluded that if this project was going to be done in time, there was no time to follow normal procedures. Even if they were willing to work weekends and holidays and around the clock, the company shut down at 5 p.m. every day. There was no time to ask permission. There was no time to file requisitions. There was no time.

During the next two weeks, various configurations were attempted, all within the "package" concept of the Najjar/Sipple car. An English Ford in-line four-cylinder engine was drawn in as part of a standard front-engine/rear-wheel-drive version. But cowl height and weight balance, though acceptable for a production coupe or sedan, did not lend themselves to a sparkling show car that was meant to advance the state of the automotive art. Frank Theyleg's Cardinal V-4 was drawn in behind the driver's seat, utilizing the same transaxle system he had developed. It fit, and the profile and its measurements looked appealing. A 1-inch steel-tube, semi-unitized space frame was designed that would incorporate the engine and transaxle as partial load- and stress-bearing elements.

On May 23, Lunn visited custom car fabricators Troutman and Barnes in Culver City, California, to arrange for them to fabricate the body. The next day, back in Dearborn, the program began. From the Najjar/Sipple full-size clay model, working drawings of the space frame were made. By June 4, these were on their way to Culver City. Meanwhile, the modelers formed a female plaster mold. From these, they created male fiberglass and resin body forms. Once these hardened, the forms were cleaned up, painted, and fitted to a body buck for wind-tunnel tests. The shape worked, and the side-mounted radiators—placed in high-pressure areas in the airstream along the car body—proved to have just enough air flow through them to cool the engine. Styling and Engineering agreed that retractable headlights were necessary to keep airflow well-managed over and around the car. Immediately after the wind-tunnel sessions, the body was shipped to Troutman and Barnes for fabrication out of aluminum panels welded together.

All this time, Styling was creating the interior. Two fixed seats were molded in one piece

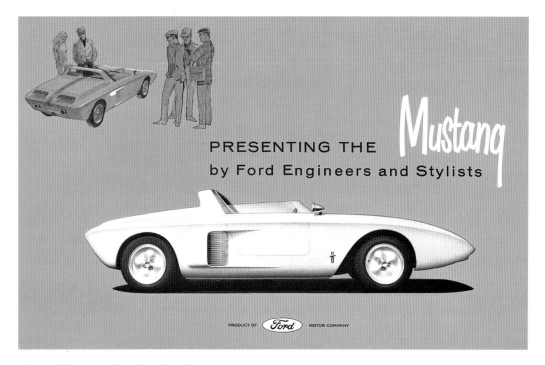

PRESENTING THE *Mustang* by Ford Engineers and Stylists

PRODUCT OF (Ford) MOTOR COMPANY

Tens of thousands of copies of this single-sheet, double-fold brochure were printed and distributed at Watkins Glen, throughout universities and engineering schools across the United States, and again at Laguna Seca to introduce the car. *Kerry Morse archives*

Next page top
In the pits at Watkins Glen, Ford test driver Danny Jones sat in the Mustang while the mechanics and the truck driver, as well as Roy Lunn (third from right with tie and glasses) and Bob Negstad (dark jacket), posed for a photograph. In the background was the transporter that Styling created to carry the car. *Bob Negstad archives*

to be mounted rigidly to the car body. This would add torsional stiffness to an already tight frame. Because the car was to be shown first at an international road race, it was designed and built as a race car. Its roll bar and other features met international race-sanctioning organization standards. Its fully independent suspension used upper and lower A-arms, front and rear, adopting then-current racing technology. Front disc brakes and large rear drums were adapted. A rack-and-pinion steering system was fitted with a flexible steering shaft. This allowed fore and aft movement of the steering wheel. Because the seats were fixed, the foot pedals adjusted to the driver. Much of this was shipped to Culver City by August 23, including a mockup of the V-4 engine and transaxle for test fitting.

While Engineering finished up chassis and engine development and Troutman and Barnes' craftsmen hand-hammered and assembled the body, Styling went to work again. A truck and trailer were withdrawn from a corporate motor pool, thoroughly cleaned, and then repainted. The trailer to transport the new car to Watkins Glen was carpeted and fitted with tool boxes.

The body and chassis got back to Dearborn on September 7. A modified V-4, similar to

the engine in production in Germany in the Taunus 12M, came from Advance Engine Engineering on September 18. On September 21, Transmissions and Drive Train delivered the transaxle. On September 23, the painted and finished body arrived from Styling, and from then until October 2, no one in the project rested. Details and finish work kept the team slaving around the clock, with only enough time out for a trip home to shower, change clothes, grab a meal, and return. Sleep, such as it was, often came on the benches and the floor around the car.

The car already had a name. Designer John Najjar had long admired the World War II fighter, the Mustang. The lines of his car design appealed to him as much as the airplane, and he felt that Engineering had produced a car worthy of the name. John Breeden, who handled public relations for Styling, ran the name past the legal department. Somewhere along the line, someone preferred the equine image of Najjar's idea over the fighter plane. The wild American horse fit everyone's concept of the car. Designer Phil Clark drew the galloping horse logo. It was added to the side of the white-painted transporter, and Breeden teased the population of Detroit with a newspaper ad announcing a new horse in Ford's corral.

On October 2, Herb Misch and Don Frey approved the completed vehicle, and it was loaded into its white-painted transporter and left for New York that afternoon.

On October 6, Gene Bordinat arrived at Watkins Glen. He was to host the press conference the next day to introduce the new Mustang as an example of the "Total Performance" concept that was "Powered by Ford." Dan Gurney drove the car out onto the racing course, and Negstad remembered hearing lap times that would have been respectable in any sports-car race at that track.

Ford printed 20,000 brochures to introduce the new Mustang and gave all of them away that weekend. To race fans and to journalists, it appeared that Ford had done something remarkable. Automotive artist Peter Helck drove the parade laps with Stirling Moss as

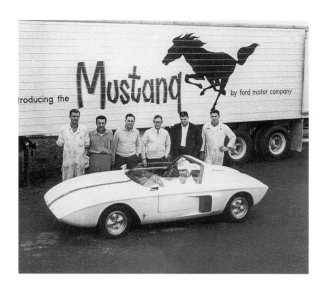

his passenger. When Dan Gurney drove pace laps before the race start in the same car, the spectators believed they were seeing the next great thing, and it was the most exciting thing any of them had ever seen from an American car maker.

Below
Following the introduction of the Mustang at Watkins Glen, Ford demonstrated the car again at Monterey, California, during sports cars races at Laguna Seca. Dan Gurney drove it once again. *Photo by Lester Nehamkin, Kerry Morse archives*

3

Cravings, Ravings, and Sleepless Nights
November 1960–October 1962

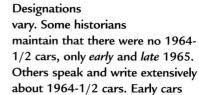

Automobile enthusiast media covered the Mustang like shrink wrap. No one was ready for the clamor that the mid-engined car created. Certainly no one expected a reaction so strong, loud, big, and favorable.

Well, perhaps Roy Lunn expected it. Maybe Hal Sperlich did. Probably Bob Negstad.

The Mustang gave Ford Motor Company something no other Ford-produced car had in several years: positive enthusiast publicity. And it gave that recognition to Iacocca.

Between mid-October and early November, magazine and newspaper writers and photographers kept the car occupied. The Mustang got cover play on the December issues of the major and minor auto magazines. The most recent Ford-powered product to garner that kind of attention had been just nine months before when Carroll Shelby's Cobras had caught the eye and the heart of car-buff writers and editors. But that, in truth, was Shelby's car, not Iacocca's. The Mustang was something that Iacocca could point to as something done on his watch. Yet it was exactly what he didn't want: a wildly favorable reaction to a two-seater.

Engineers involved in the project were freed up from other assignments, and they took the Mustang on tour across the United States. It appeared in major auto shows from New York to Los Angeles. After the shows, it began a college tour. It went to Florida and Georgia; Roy Lunn began one leg at Purdue University in early April. Helmut Graetzel went on with the car to Penn State University, and Lunn was back with the car at Carnegie Institute of Technology two days later. Bob Negstad took the West Coast leg, visiting Stanford, the University of California at Berkeley, and both the University of California, Los Angeles (UCLA) and the University of Southern California (USC) in a six-day frenzy. Len Bailey went with the car to the University of Illinois at Champaign-Urbana on May 8; Norm Postma went to Northwestern University May 10. On one tour alone, they visited seventeen universities where there were mechanical or automotive engineering schools and student chapters of the Society of Automotive Engineers (SAE). Another 30,000 brochures were printed and given away. They and the car showed up—sometimes unannounced just to gauge spontaneous reaction—driving it onto college campuses from coast to coast. It created traffic jams. The car was constantly—and sometimes instantly—mobbed.

Publication clipping services that monitored newspapers and magazines for mention of Ford's products in print were filling oversize envelops each week to send back to the Ford Division public affairs office. Several scrapbooks were fattened. Ford Engineering took advantage of the frenzy and used the Mustang as an opportunity to recruit top engineering candidates. Everywhere that the engineers and the Mustang traveled, people wanted to know when it would be available and how much it would cost. No one seemed concerned that the car had no roof or that it seated only two. People simply wanted the car.

Back in Dearborn, Roy Lunn had nearly concluded his vigorous campaign to put the two-seater into production. He had commissioned a detailed analysis of the specifications and features of the sports-car competition from around the world. His presentation compared Porsche, Alfa Romeo, MG, Triumph, Fiat, and Sunbeam. The Mustang compared favorably in most ways. In

Designations
vary. Some historians maintain that there were no 1964-1/2 cars, only *early* and *late* 1965. Others speak and write extensively about 1964-1/2 cars. Early cars became "late" on August 18, 1964. Before that date, cars had generators. Afterward, production replaced them with alternators and fit a warning light with a lens reading ALT.

Opposite
1964-1/2 Mustang hardtop
This was the final result of Lee Iacocca's Fairlane Committee dinners in Dearborn. Designed by Dave Ash in the Ford styling studio, it was first called the Cougar. Its lines were first introduced to Ford Division management as a clay model in mid-August 1962.

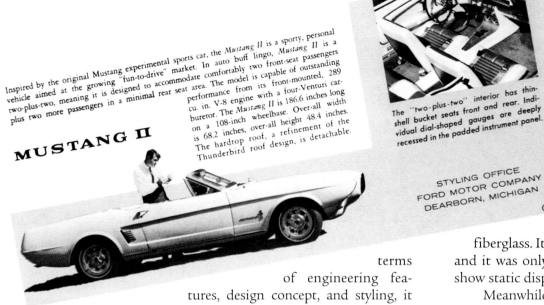

Inspired by the original Mustang experimental sports car, the *Mustang II* is a sporty, personal vehicle aimed at the growing "fun-to-drive" market. In auto buff lingo, Mustang II is a two-plus-two, meaning it is designed to accommodate comfortably two front-seat passengers plus two more passengers in a minimal rear seat area. The model is capable of outstanding performance from its front-mounted, 289 cu. in. V-8 engine with a four-Venturi carburetor. The *Mustang II* is 186.6 inches long on a 108-inch wheelbase. Over-all width is 68.2 inches, over-all height 48.4 inches. The hardtop roof, a refinement of the Thunderbird roof design, is detachable.

MUSTANG II

The "two-plus-two" interior has thin-shell bucket seats front and rear. Individual dial-shaped gauges are deeply recessed in the padded instrument panel.

STYLING OFFICE
FORD MOTOR COMPANY
DEARBORN, MICHIGAN

To put out the fire ignited by the first Mustang mid-engined car, Lee Iacocca asked Styling to produce a 1963 functional show car that carried over many of the visual cues of the two-seater while making it clear that this car was to seat four. It was named the Mustang II and was often shown in conjunction with the Allegro, the Styling proposal that led to the production Mustang. Bob Negstad archives

Because the Mustang not only functioned completely but because it did it so well, it stunned the magazine writers. During the same Grand Prix weekend, Chevrolet introduced its Corvair Monza GT. While GM employees pushed the show car from one display area to the next, the Mustang was out running laps as the official pace car for the race. (A second Mustang was assembled later, made of fiberglass. It did not have an engine/transaxle, and it was only a push-around model for auto-show static displays.)

Meanwhile, back at the corral, work had continued on a number of prototypes. The direction clearly was leading to two doors and four seats. To back up a bit, Iacocca had gone to Henry Ford II in mid-1962 to propose a new car program to produce the four-seater, but there was little interest. The Falcon Sprint had failed to meet its sales expectations, due in part to its coming through at a sale price about $600 higher than the Corvair Monza, even though it was fitted with fewer standard features. Dealers couldn't give them away and would not stop screaming about it. Committing corporate funds to a new four-passenger sporty car seemed ill-advised in view of the sales performance of its predecessor.

Styling too seemed to be moving along at less than top speed. Iacocca was impatient. He wanted this car, and he had come to believe in it, whatever it might look like. Corvair's Monza continued to sell, and his old friends in dealerships called him personally to complain. The mid-engined Mustang show car was still in the works at this point, and it would go out to promote a car that—as yet—no one had even designed. He told Bordinat that he wanted a contest to design the car, as a way to challenge the designers and stylists from Ford and Lincoln-Mercury divisions and from Advanced Corporate Projects. His deadline was two weeks. When the eraser dust settled and the designers stumbled through the detritus of crumpled vellum, crushed cigarettes, and

terms of engineering features, design concept, and styling, it motored far ahead of the field. Charlie Maddox and Norm Postma prepared a paper for Lunn to present to the SAE during its national convention held in Detroit in mid-January 1963. By that time, however, Ford division management had begun to make it very clear that the car was not going to be produced. The title of Lunn's paper was "The Mustang—Ford's Experimental Sports Car." Iacocca characterized it as something "to show the kids that they should wait for us because we had some good, hot stuff coming."

"The *corporation* never did decide to build *that* car," Bob Negstad recalled more than thirty years after the Watkins Glen showing. "That was done by the guys over in Research and Advanced Vehicles, who had this task of showing a car, 'powered by Ford.' That got lost.

"That's been lost all these years. The reason [the car was built] was to . . . to tell the people that Ford Engineering had new engines, and the engines were exciting. And boy, that just got completely pushed to the sidelines." Negstad smiled. He was one of the engineers who did a little of the nudging. "We took the engine engineering and we moved it right out onto wheels and tires and brakes and suspension. We expanded on that theme a lot more than anyone thought we were gonna do. Most Styling cars are just push-arounds, they're good for photography. But not functional. And that Mustang was completely, totally functional."

failed drawings, Dave Ash, an assistant to Ford Styling's studio head Joe Oros, was the winner. Ash named his car the Cougar.

The Cougar almost exaggerated the long-hood and short rear deck-lid approach as stylists worked hard to reverse the appearance trends of the Falcon and the newer Fairlane. The Cougar was striking and simple. Ash's driver's side door carried over the long sculpted scoop that had led cooling air to the midship radiators on the Najjar/Sipple Mustang.

On September 10, 1962, Iacocca went again to see Henry Ford II to pitch the production of Ash's Cougar design. Ford Motor Company President Arjay Miller, another of the Whiz Kids hired at the same time as McNamara, had commissioned an estimate of how many cars the company would sell. The report would take into account the numbers of customers switching from Falcon, Fairlane, and other Ford models, but its goal was to find the number of additional cars that would be sold beyond that. Corporate research head George Brown produced a figure of 86,000, not really enough to justify the cost. But Henry Ford II had come to like the idea of the car, and Iacocca had made his notes at home and did his salesman-best at work to emphasize that this car, using mostly Falcon pieces, could go into production quickly and at reasonable cost. Ford agreed, at last. He gave Iacocca $40 million to do it and a target date of March 9, 1964, for Job One, the first cars to drive off the assembly line. Public introduction would be five weeks later. This meant Iacocca had barely eighteen months to reach Job One, a period that was about half as long as usual.

Iacocca had settled on Dave Ash's Cougar body more than six months before Ford's long-sought approval. Of course, now that the car was given the go-ahead, the thousand small details

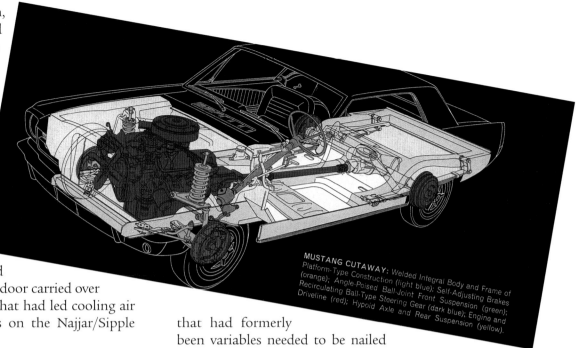

MUSTANG CUTAWAY: Welded Integral Body and Frame of Platform-Type Construction (light blue); Self-Adjusting Brakes (orange); Angle-Poised Ball-Joint Front Suspension (green); Recirculating Ball-Type Steering Gear (dark blue); Engine and Driveline (red); Hypoid Axle and Rear Suspension (yellow).

that had formerly been variables needed to be nailed down. And, the car had to be made to move and turn and stop.

The foundation of the production car, still called the Cougar, or referred to by its in-house code designation as the T-5, was basically the Falcon Sprint. Nothing invented for Roy Lunn's Mustang prototype was going to be carried over into production. That technology would go elsewhere—with Lunn and later with Chuck Mountain, Len Bailey, Bud Anderson, Jim Graham, Bob Mahew, Bob Negstad, and others, to England and on into racing.

The Sprint seemed like a good departure point. Shortly after the introduction of McNamara's Falcon for the 1960 model year, Chevrolet had turned the tables on economy cars by introducing its Monza performance option on its Corvair. Ford had been caught napping, and the Monza was its wake-up call. Improved—dramatically improved—performance became a high priority for the Falcon.

Dearborn Steel Tubing (DST) was a company that for years had done custom fabrication and modification for Ford Motor Company for evaluation and modeling purposes. They were asked to put the new Fairlane 221ci V-8 into the Falcon.

"Jim White and Andy Hotten and their guys at DST went away," Bob Negstad explained, "and

This cut-away appeared in the first sales brochures for the early 1965 (or 1964-1/2) Mustang. The oversize brochure was lushly designed, lavishly illustrated, and expensively printed to send a message to buyers that this car offered unexpected features and value to its buyers. *Bob Negstad archives*

The first regular production Mustang, a Wimbledon white V-8 convertible, was sold to a Canadian airline pilot. He ultimately traded it back to Ford for a new model in March 1966, the 1 millionth car produced. The pilot's first car ended up in the Henry Ford Museum & Greenfield Village. This car, the second produced, was purchased by a family whose name is no longer known—a typical situation with the second of anything.

came back in nothing flat with a V-8 stuffed into a Falcon. They patched it up and put it in. Drove it around and, by golly! It felt like a Falcon with a little V-8 in it.

"'Oh boy! This is our answer to the Monza.' I heard people say that!" Negstad recalled. "So Ford continued with the V-8, and it wound up being the Falcon Sprint."

"It broke this and broke that," he continued. "Along the way, a lot of Fairlane parts got adapted to the Sprint. They borrowed the front spindle so they could borrow the front brakes. The Falcon was designed for 6.00x13-inch tires and 13x4-inch wheels, and it had 9-inch brake drums. And those were just totally inadequate for anything other than, say, parking it when you were shopping. None of that was gonna work with a V-8 in the car.

"So Fairlane parts kept going into the Falcon. More Fairlane parts. A bigger sector shaft on the steering. It picked up, oh, the axle out of the Fairlane. It picked up the transmission and clutch parts. And the radiator. And . . ."

Negstad speaks in syncopation. He has a sense of when to wait two beats for dramatic timing and when it's better to just machine gun ahead.

"Oh, on and on and on. When they got all done, bottom line was the Falcon Sprint was nothing like a Falcon. It was, for all practical purposes, a re-mix of parts off the shelf from other car lines, mainly Fairlane. To share components made the Falcon into a viable alternative. It came out too expensive but . . ."

Enter Hal Sperlich. Sperlich had been brought in to Ford to develop the idea of product planning. A founding member of Iacocca's Fairlane Committee, Sperlich, who worked as special projects assistant for Don Frey, has been characterized as being very bright and very intelligent, if somewhat retrospective.

"Sperlich saw this Falcon Sprint," Negstad remembered, "and the fact that Ford had spent a fortune tooling and modifying it and couldn't give it away. All the tools were there, bought and paid for. And he saw the success of the small sporty, two-passenger Mustang, and he said, 'Whoa, here's an opportunity. Take the Falcon Sprint, re-skin it, re-do it, re-trim it, and re-pre-

The airline pilot who bought the first car went for the V-8. The family that purchased this model chose economy and specified the 170-cubic-inch, in-line six-cylinder originally developed for the Falcon. It produced 101 horsepower at 4,400 rpm and 156 foot-pounds of torque at 2,400 rpm. This was the base model engine for the Mustang, and it was coupled to a three-speed manual transmission.

sent it as a sporty car.'" Sperlich put together a think tank, from Product Study Vehicles, to conceive of new packages for the Falcon Sprint.

"Everybody was given a different scheme," Negstad explained. "My assignment was to try to put the six-cylinder engine behind the seat, transversely mounted and make a rear-engine/rear-wheel-drive Falcon. Really! The only one that made any sense at all was to take a Falcon Sprint just like it was. Take everything off that Sprint and throw it away. Get rid of it. Peel off the fenders. Peel off the doors. Put on new fenders. And doors. And there's your car. Put on a body that didn't look anything like a Falcon Sprint.

"The Falcon Sprint had a short nose and a long tail. Fine, we'll make a short tail and a long nose. Gene Bordinat and [Advance Design Director Don] DeLaRossa's people did that. And it turns out, it looked pretty good. And it was faithful to being the cost of a face-lift. When they 'costed' it—what it cost to build it—it was

peanuts. Quick peanuts! And the Mustang was born. It borrowed the emblem. And the name."

It was mid-September 1962. Less than a week after the biggest sale of Lee Iacocca's career—the Cougar to Henry Ford II for nothing down and $40 million over eighteen months—full-size drawings were made from Dave Ash's clay model. Eighteen months later when the car would appear, it would be closer to its stylist's original idea than any Ford that had come before it. Everyone involved with the project—from Henry Ford II down to the newest engineering trainee—came to like the car so much that many of the usual conflicts simply didn't happen. This is not to say there were not glitches, problems, and arguments over pedal placement, front- and rear-suspension travel, the typeface to be used for the car's name, the car's name itself, battery placement, roll-up rear quarter windows, the direction of the logo, and the stitching style to be used on the upholstery. But there was a feeling about the car, that it was right, that it had possibilities, and that those possibilities could make for an exciting future at Ford.

Surveys, market research, and viewer tests went on at an accelerated pace. The trends that Chase Morsey, Bob Eggert, and Frank Zimmerman had cited in Fairlane Committee meetings had been reinforced by further studies and by practical observation. Younger buyers *were* coming into the dealerships. The gross national product and real wages were rising. And starting salaries for new college graduates entering their first jobs were higher than ever.

A number of product surveys gave groups of people a chance to see a mockup of the new car and to estimate its price based on the features that were listed. Consistently, people overestimated this figure—in some cases by as much as three times its projected introductory price. When they made this assessment, they looked longingly—but distantly—at the car. When they learned it could be sold for less than $2,500, they immediately began to think of ways they *could* afford it and reasons they *should* have it. At less than $2,500, this car was not an unapproachable luxury; it became a practical form of transportation that offered unmatched style and flair.

This encouragement provoked Ford division management to rethink initial sales projections. It was one thing to produce a failure that didn't sell up to expectations and to be stuck with unwanted inventory. It was another to fail because you produced a product that exceeded expectations but for which you had insufficient inventory. By the summer of 1963, Iacocca was convinced that Ford would sell more than 200,000 cars. As the educated predictions continued, Iacocca went to the corporation to ask for more production capacity, for what he believed might be a first-year sale of 360,000 cars. They accepted his judgment, and the San Jose, California, plant was prepared for conversion. Just before spring of 1964, the Metuchen, New Jersey, plant was converted as well.

The question of the car's name kept coming up. Dave Ash's boss, Joe Oros, sent notes to Iacocca throughout the fall of 1962, encouraging him to keep the name "Cougar." But historically, at Ford Motor Company, automobile names had been proposed by its ad agency. In their thoroughness, the J. Walter Thompson agency submitted a list containing 6,000 possibilities for this new car. Somehow that was narrowed down to a final six: Cougar, Bronco, Puma, Cheeta, Colt, and Mustang. By November 1962, Mustang was chosen because of its suggestion of moving fast through open country.

Later—as late as January 1964—the car was still called, variously, the Special Falcon, the Cougar, T-5, the Mustang, and even the Torino—a name introduced to honor Iacocca's heritage. The J. Walter Thompson agency was preparing advertising copy, shooting brochure photographs, writing press releases and television advertising scripts, and still the name was being played with. The flood of publicity surrounding the mid-engine Mustang still swirled around Ford. While a few individuals had been invited to participate in surveys and had gotten to see—without being told specifically—what the 1964-1/2 car would look like, letters still got to Public Affairs, Styling, Engineering and even to Ford World Headquarters asking for the two-seater.

Iacocca felt it was necessary to both turn down the fire that was boiling under the two-seat enthusiasts and to redirect the show car's publicity towards something more akin to what was in the works. A pre-production prototype was deliv-ered to DST with the directions to modify it. Mustang II, as it was to be called, would clearly retain its four-seat identity but should pick up some of the styling cues of the two-seater, now known as Mustang I. It was painted white with a blue racing stripe and blue interior, as Mustang I had been. Fiberglass was added to the front and rear to restyle the nose and tail, and a slightly modified roof line gave the impression that the car was much lower and longer than the 5 inches it actually was lengthened.

Mustang II was introduced on the October 6, 1963, Watkins Glen Grand Prix weekend. It met Iacocca's objective of cooling the passion for a two-seater, but it did little to dampen the enthusiasm that had grown for Ford's "Total Performance" program. The race weekend crowd picked up brochures, and many asked "When?" with the same anxious interest as they had the previous year for Mustang I.

But a serious problem appeared late in 1963. The early driveable prototypes were breaking.

"The first Mustangs," Bob Negstad explained, "were put together and sent out on 'durability.' Potholes. And they destroyed themselves. The body structure was terrible. They broke up under 'durability.'"

The only options the economy-minded original buyers of this car agreed to were a push-button AM radio (a $57.51 option), floor mats ($4.85), and imitation wire wheels with knock-off hubs ($17.82.). Base price of the car itself was $2,320.96. All prices were in U.S. dollars, of course.

The Mustang sat on a 108-inch wheelbase and measured 181.6 inches long overall. It stood 51.1 inches tall, 68.2 inches wide, and weighed 2,562 pounds. Its trunk was a modest 8.9 cubic-feet while its gasoline capacity was 16.0 gallons.

Negstad paused for his two beats.

"And there was a relatively small group of people that did this development part, the Make-A-Mustang-Out-Of-The-Falcon-Sprint group. And when the car started to have trouble, everybody scattered. And ran. And disappeared. And went away. And they said, 'Oh my God. Here's a disaster.'"

"The few people that were the real movers and shakers behind the car—Hal Sperlich and Lee Iacocca—and the people that were stuck with this Mustang deal, we knew we had to fix it. Bob Stone worked on the body structure of the Falcon, the Falcon Sprint, and the Mustang; his plan was simple.

He said to me, 'We're going to do the work to make a convertible. We're going to *make* a convertible.' To fix the problem, Bob Stone added the convertible structure to the base vehicle. Torque boxes front and rear, front rail reinforcements, rocker box upgrades, changes in number three cross-member, and other modifications to the floor pan.

"So we added the structure to make a convertible. And did all the testing. And the evaluating. And the twisting. And the durability. We did all that on the convertible as well. Fixed the convertible.

"Came down to the coupe . . . piece of cake. Put a top on a convertible, and you've got even more stiffness. Piece of cake, just a piece of cake. The Mustang coupe was almost *too* stiff," Negstad chuckled. "And that was a cost reduction, from '64 1/2 to the '65. Remove some parts."

As the car got closer to production, a number of pleasant surprises occurred. The efforts to keep costs down had succeeded. Doing such things as fundamental as creating only one line of Mustang in coupe, convertible, and by the fall of 1964, a fastback—rather than a sport model, standard version, and a luxury model, each with different names, badges, sales brochures, and promotion and advertising expenses—had returned money to the division for other uses.

The selling price was announced as $2,368, an odd figure with a curious—and easily remembered—ring to it. With some extra money available for each car, they all got full-size hubcaps; full carpeting; bucket seats; front armrests; a cigarette lighter; padded dash; self-adjusting brakes; a sport steering wheel; a three-speed, floor-mounted gear shift; bumper guards front and rear; automatic door courtesy lights; and a glove box light. Many buyers would remember April 17 as the first time they ever saw such an affordable car so thoroughly equipped at no extra cost.

This was coupled with an option list that offered to upgrade the standard in-line 170 cubic-inch, 101 horsepower, six-cylinder engine to a 260 or 289 cubic-inch V-8; to replace the three-speed with a four-speed stick shift or a T-bar Cruise-O-Matic automatic transmission; to make available power brakes and steering and a power top for the convertible; air conditioning; tinted glass; vinyl roof covering; 14-inch wire wheel covers or 15-inch sport wheels and tires; and nearly a dozen other options before the buyer ever saw the color chart.

However, throughout the winter of 1963 and into the early spring of 1964, leading up to the introduction, one more concern crept into the minds at Ford management, Engineering, and Styling. Recent experience with another product that had received so much pre-production interest was beginning to worry some of the participants. Few people were willing to mention the "E" car, but the similarities were becoming alarming.

Ford management had learned a great deal from the Edsel disaster. Introduced in September 1957, the Edsel followed careful research which confirmed that buyers existed for an upper-middle-market car, something between the Mercury and Lincoln. Its standard equipment included self-adjusting brakes and an automatic transmission shifted by push-buttons in the center of the steering wheel. But advertising hype got going on the E-car, and by the time of its introduction, consumers crowded the showrooms expecting to see the wheel reinvented, a better mouse trap, an improved bread slicer, and if the car had a halo, that wouldn't have been entirely unexpected.

Instead, the Edsel had a startling front end, four wheels and tires, and it was outfitted with a pretty conventional array of features—albeit all as standard equipment—but conventional nonetheless. It had chrome and striking two-tone paint combinations. But it couldn't fly or float or improve the buyers' marriages or even fix their breakfast. Other factors also contributed. There was an entry-level and an upper-level Edsel, with a confusing structure of lower and higher prices but barely discernible differences in styling. What's more, an economic recession in 1958 undermined the buying public for the pricier luxury version. In all, Ford Motor Company lost perhaps as much as $250 million creating, developing, promoting, and killing the E-car.

After all its buildup, after all the publicity, after all the research done to confirm the buying public's hunger for such a vehicle, would this new four-seater become known as the M-car?

The first five Mustangs were shipped by Ford Division to Ford of Canada for display and demonstration. All five cars ultimately ended up sold in the eastern provinces. Back in early April 1964, these cars were nothing more than new models of an unproven make. It was only afterward, when the phenomenal sales records were set and the period of history became known as the "pony car" era that historians recognized that the first—and even the second—car had significance.

4

Total Frenzy— Powered by Ford
1964-1/2–1966

The M-car registered 22,000 sales the first day. By the close of business, December 31, 1964, Ford had sold 263,434 Mustangs, and as the sun rose in Dearborn on April 17, 1965, Iacocca's sporty four-seater had sold 418,812 cars during its first year. Iacocca had beaten Robert McNamara's Falcon sales record by 1,638 cars.

It had all been carefully orchestrated. From the first of Iacocca's Fairlane Committee dinners, he continued to write in his black book, and he left his good people alone to do their job. In the end, the only modification necessary was to change Iacocca's motto from "Total Performance."

It became "Mustang Mania."

On March 2, 1964 a week before Job One, and forty-five days before the official launch date, Walter Buhl Ford II snuck out from Dearborn to lunch in downtown Detroit in a black Mustang convertible, one of the 150 pre-release cars built to de-bug the production lines. Fred Olmsted with the Detroit Free Press noticed the car, called a staff photographer who came quickly and shot pictures. These moved over the wire services, and newspapers and news magazines nationwide got an advanced look. Did Henry Ford II punish his nephew Walter? Or promote him?

The previous fall, Ford public affairs had invited magazine writers to Dearborn for a day-long briefing. Hal Sperlich outlined for them the influences and the studies that had dictated and shaped the new car. Lee Iacocca emphasized the sporty nature of the car that would be, at the same time, very economical. The following January many of the same writers were invited back for "ride-and-drive" sessions around the Dearborn handling track in pre-production models. Dealers in thirteen major North American cities saw live musical stage shows that introduced the car and built support and excitement. Months later, just before the introduction, Ford mailed 11,000 press kits to newspapers and magazines in Canada, the United States, Puerto Rico, and Mexico.

On Monday, April 13, four days before the public introduction, Ford hosted 150 journalists at the New York World's Fair. After leading them on a tour of Ford's Pavilion, Iacocca again explained the nature and the history of the car they would be seeing in several days. They all adjourned to a luncheon whereupon the 150 startled writers were handed keys to seventy-five new Mustangs and released to drive themselves back to Dearborn. Later that evening, Walter Hoving, chairman of Tiffany and Company, presented Henry Ford II with the Tiffany Gold Medal Award, "for excellence in American design." The Mustang was the first automobile ever to be so honored.

At 9:30 P.M. on Thursday, April 16, Ford aired what may have been some of television's first infomercials, unveiling the new Mustang simultaneously on ABC, CBS, and NBC in a series of commercials. Ford had bought the time exclusively on the three networks, and the Neilsen ratings indicated that something like 29 million viewers saw the car first in their own living rooms.

The media blitz continued Friday morning and throughout the weekend in 2,600 newspapers with stories and paid advertisements. By the time most Ford dealers opened their doors on Friday morning, April 17, crowds surrounded their stores. A dealer in Pittsburgh had his only Mustang up on the wash rack when the crowd found it. It remained

Functional vents expelled interior air. Flaps inside the car above the back seat could be slid open or closed to control airflow. In the late afternoon, the rich rangoon red paint on the fastback 2+2 plays games with the reflections of clouds and trees.

Opposite
For 1966, the fastback 2+2 sold for $2,607.07, an increase of not quite $54.00. The slight rise in price didn't slow sales at all as total production for 1966 rose to 607,568 even though Fastback numbers fell from 77,079 to 35,698. The biggest gain was in hardtop production, from 409,260 up 20 percent to 499,751.

Newsweek **magazine cover featured Iacocca and his new car.** *Tony Navarra archives*

1966 GT Fastback

The 1966 models, including the two-door convertible GT and two-door Fastback 2+2, differed only very slightly from the 1965 cars. The sales brochures even confirmed it: "Relax, Mustang lovers. Your favorite car hasn't changed much for 1966."

there all day because the crowd never thinned out enough for him to remove it and drive it into the showroom. A Texas dealer sold his last floor sample to the highest bidder, who insisted on sleeping in the car overnight while the bank cleared his check. Mustangs were displayed in banks, in airports, and in hotels and shopping centers. Convertibles in Wimbledon White were provided as official pace cars (some sources report two, others say three were built) for the 48th Annual Indianapolis 500-mile race. The official cars were equipped with performance and handling modifications in addition to what was provided in the 289 cubic-inch engine's "Hi-Po" high-performance option. Another 190 coupes and thirty-five convertibles—also in Wimbledon White—were provided as pace-car replicas to 1964 race officials. All the replicas, however, were equipped with the 260 V-8.

Ford's idea with the publicity and media blitz was to put the car in front of everyone in North America. Iacocca was sure that once they saw the car—and realized its price—they would want it and they would buy it. That was part of the sales and marketing strategy. All the advertising and even its luxurious full-color sales brochure presented its "Unexpected Look!", its "Unexpected Price!", its "Unexpected Choice!" of options, and its "Unexpected Versatility!" The large 11x10in brochure was expensively produced on heavy paper with elegant photography that was routine with a $7,000 or $8,000 Lincoln but was unexpected with a $2,368 economy car.

Television commercials made it clear that radical personality changes occurred in Mustang buyers, turning them from shy, retiring individuals into lively, interesting, and exciting human beings. Women and men figured equally in the commercials, as they had in all the marketing surveys and planning from the first Fairlane Committee meetings. From the start, it was meant that this car should appeal in equal measure to female buyers as well as males.

It worked nearly too well. Something like 16,000 Mustangs had been produced during the

six weeks before the official introduction date—around 535 per day from the Dearborn Assembly Plant, beginning March 9. And by the end of the first day of sales, Ford Motor Company was already some 6,000 cars behind. (The San Jose plant wasn't up and running until early July, according to the *Mustang Production Guide, Vol 1, '65-66*, and San Jose then quickly changed over to 1965-model year production. Metuchen would not be in operation until February 1965.)

It was almost a problem. Supply always slightly lagged demand. It was the best kind of problem to Ford and Iacocca. Dealers were selling all the cars they could get. In some cases, deliveries were subject to delays as long as eight weeks. Yet customers waited. The Financial Production Volume—that is, the number of cars that needed to be sold to pay for the project's tooling—was met within the first six months. This meant that the Mustang was profitable shortly after its 1965 models were introduced. While the hardtop was base priced at $2,320.96, most cars were sold with options that ran the delivered price up to around $3,000. Dealers—and Ford Division—made even more money from the options.

Some people within the company deservedly stood around patting themselves on the back. But many more stared into their morning coffee cups and read inter-office sales reports and wondered how it had happened. How they could have done it without them?

The late Ken Purdy, one of America's finest automotive writers once said, "Great cars are designed by small groups of dedicated people." That was especially true with Mustang I, and it was equally true with the 1964-1/2 production car. Author Gary Witzenburg quoted development engineer C.N. Reuter who recalled the trouble he had getting cooperation from some of the other divisions that were meant to supply parts to the Mustang program. As Lunn and Negstad and others had experienced on the Mustang I, there was a forced-march mentality among those involved with the T-5/Cougar program. Yet among all the outside divisions and suppliers, things still had to be done through channels, with requisitions, providing the proper number of copies, and signed off with authorization. So instead, Styling and Engineering personnel called

in favors and got the car done. Just as it had been with Mustang I, once decisions were made, there was no time for second guessing.

"When you're faced with seventeen months from styling approval to Job One," Reuter told Witzenburg, "you do it the way you think it's going to work out the first time, because you don't have any room for alternatives.

"It was an interesting program," he added, "and if it hadn't been so short, I think we would have made more mistakes."

That was the sentiment voiced into coffee cups. There was little to criticize. And little reason now for outside advice. So, of course, it came. Now that the car was out in the marketplace, more voices were heard.

"There was no question about the Mustang being a tremendous success," Bob Negstad recalled. "But right away there was an effort to move the car upscale. Right away.

"A planning paper came along," he continued, "where they said, 'We want to do a super-deluxe interior, with leather and built-in air-conditioning in the dash, not a hang on. And we want to do, oh, higher series wheels and tires.' And they had a whole long list of items to move the car toward what would be an upscale, more personalized, popular car . . . would be a Thunderbird. They produced a dollar figure and an investment figure to accomplish this.

"So, we offered an alternate proposal. 'If you want to upscale the car, let's upscale in two directions,' we said. 'Yes, a luxury car, that's fine. But we ought to take the Mustang towards some of its original concept because we've said all along there's a market out there for the enthusiasts' point of view.'

"They said okay!"

Negstad's proposal included several items. Ford had become an industry leader with its disc brakes after Holman and Moody built the Falcon's for the Monte Carlo rally. The V-8-powered Falcons couldn't stop with their small drum brakes. To satisfy the sanctioning body's rules for Falcon Futura at Monte Carlo, a thousand cars had to be produced with matching specification. Ford ordered 10,000 sets of disc brakes, and Falcon won its class in 1963. All the engineers wanted to use those brakes on the performance-ver-

Showroom-new is the appearance to the naked eye. But within the confines of the cast iron and chrome there is a Jack Roush-modified 289 that is producing something closer to 350 horsepower than the showroom-new 271 horsepower that all other owners have to live with. The two-piece brace between the shock towers served to stiffen the front end of the chassis to improve handling.

sion Mustang. And Negstad wanted an independent rear suspension.

"They said, 'Well, okay . . . but!'" Negstad again waited two beats. "'Don't touch the structure. Don't change the body.'"

The chassis engineers set out to design something like a major sub-assembly. This way the production line could just wrench it onto the car in the same way that they put in the solid rear axle. When the engineers had invented it and assembled it, with its rear disc brakes, the entire structure fit into existing bolt locations with the addition of only three new holes.

"So Assembly would bolt this in, bolt that in, bolt that other thing in. Everything else goes up on the car and bolts on wherever it used to," Negstad continued. The engineers recommended that every new frame be manufactured with the three new holes, but only those cars with the independent rear suspensions (IRS) would need them.

"That was the gist of it. Bolt it up and drive it down the road. We wound up manufacturing two of these cars. They were a delight. We had a version with brakes inboard and a version with brakes outboard. Used Armstrong adjustable shock absorbers all around.

"We even featured a cast wheel. I went out and talked to Ted Halibrand and bought a set of patterns. Made these magnesium wheels for the project . . ."

For Negstad, as part of a small group of dedicated people, the IRS project was one of his early disappointments. The IRS was killed for several reasons that came from inside the company and outside the state. Other projects with greater perceived benefit could better use the money. And times were changing. Projects could no longer be initiated by small groups, they had to come from larger groups, and preferably those groups would incorporate a few other departments besides only Engineering and Styling.

The two coupe prototypes with the independent rear suspensions and four-wheel disc brakes are preserved in storage in suburban Detroit. Negstad's magnesium wheel patterns were picked up by Avanti.

One element that came out of the IRS project was adopted into "mainstream" Ford planning. It had been born, in fact, during work on the Mustang I. It was a technique—even a philosophy—for doing suspension geometry, invented by a young Ford engineer and computer wizard named Chuck Carrig. He was a master of Fortran, one of the languages of computer programming in the early 1960s.

"Chuck was trying to sell his boss on the idea of using computer-generated models to do suspension geometry," Negstad remembered. "He believed you could do four-bar linkages with computers. This was 1961.

"Management laughed. 'Okay, kid,' they said, 'we use it for payroll, and it's good to keep track of inventory, but . . .'

"Carrig tried to tell them. 'No, no, no! You can do geometry with the thing. It'll solve the sine and cosines and tangents. It'll do positions.'

"He struggled mightily to sell his concept of using computers to generate geometries," Negstad continued. "He finally got someone to let him try but after he started to write simple programs for short-long-arm (SLA) suspensions, everybody said, 'Yeah. But how do you know it's right?'

"We were both young kids. Didn't have a jug or a rug, or a window [jargon for carpeted executive offices with coffee thermoses and windows with views]. So I started working lunch times and at night, and I'd take his four-bar linkages, and I'd lay out the geometry four-times size. And he'd run them on his computer, and I'd run lines on the papers. And usually I got done before him.

"Everybody said to us, 'Well, why do you even want to mess with that computer? He can beat you with a pencil.'"

In the early 1960s, Ford's computer was located on the top floor of the Scientific Laboratory building, running the full length of the building from the center aisle to the outside walls. Mallory vacuum tubes in rows and rows did the computing. Binary computation meant that the vacuum tubes did or did not pass the electric current. In simple terms, computing capacity was determined by the number of tubes inside the computer and how much power was available to heat up the gasses within them.

"To do this program," Negstad went on, "Chuck and I sat down one day, and we numbered the suspension points. To this day, point five and point six are the upper and lower ball joints. And point ten is ground contact.

"Well, what we discovered was that if I was right, so was Chuck's program. We'd type out the IBM cards, find some time on the computer, run it through, de-brief it, de-bug it, and we found out that it was accurate. Chuck Carrig was the guy that worked this all out, that perfected this technique to do computer modeling. It was called Program 1493.

"And when it came time to do the Mustang suspensions, we were in a hurry. And so I said, 'Hell, let's put the points on the computer and let Chuck run them out.'

"And bang! He ran them out and down he came. So I thought, 'Well, gee, let's do some variations. Let's move this and move that. Try this and try these points.' And several hours later, there it was!"

Several hours? Negstad chuckled at the memories.

"Pretty soon, everybody began to like the computer results because you could make changes without rolling out another piece of paper. That was back when you did your drawings on vellum and you had to stretch it overnight to let it absorb the moisture out of the air so that when you came in the next morning the paper

was conditioned. Then you could stretch it and grid it and start your drawing . . .

"Or, you could let Chuck run it through the 1493 program. And of course when the computers got faster . . ."

The independent rear suspension was meant to turn the Fastback 2+2 into a true European-style GT car. Gene Bordinat's stylists had already conceived of the fastback idea by mid-winter of 1963. Styling kept the project under wraps until a full-size clay model was ready in early May, and then Iacocca was invited in to see it.

Above and below
This was the proposed independent rear suspension system for the Mustang 2+2 GT. A benefit of the proposal was the addition of disc brakes to the rear axle. *Photos by Bob Negstad*

This is one of the tags that tells the history of the car. The other is usually located on the driver's-side inner fender panel. Inside the car, a Pony Interior complemented the GT five-instrument cluster along with the supplemental Rally-Pac instruments. A full-length console divided the front bucket seats.

Top right
Rear backup lights were made standard equipment for 1966, accounting for about $10 of that $54 increase. Racing team owner/car builder Jack Roush's personal transport wears a license plate that is the perquisite of being an automobile manufacturer in Michigan.

"That's what I want," he exclaimed. "Go!"

Development began that day and production started in the San Jose and Rouge plants on August 1, 1964, with introduction on September 25, as a 1965 model.

The magazines that had praised the coupe and convertible fell in love all over again. The rekindled passion was justified. Even without Negstad's IRS, the fastback handled better due to the extra mass of the sheet metal and the vast back window weighting down the rear wheels. While one or two hard-noses had criticized the non functional side scoops behind the doors, no one could say a word about the louvers in the fastback side panels that brought air into the rear seating area.

An innovative, fold-down rear seat increased storage room greatly. It turned the 2+2 back into a two-seater with enough luggage capacity for a month on the road. Other suspension, handling, and powertrain options furthered Iacocca's "Total Performance" claim.

Coupled with the 271 horsepower, high-performance 289 cubic-inch engine, buyers could order the GT Equipment group that had been introduced on April 17, 1965. Available at first for either the coupe or convertible, the package specified either the 271 horsepower or 225 horsepower engine and provided the Special Handling Package. This fitted stiffer front and rear springs and larger diameter shock absorbers, a larger front anti-sway bar, and 16:1 steering instead of the stock 19:1. Within the grille, a pair of fog lights set off the front end, and stripes below the door sill clearly announced sportier intentions. The package also provided front disc brakes and, among many other features, brought the engine exhaust out through the rear bodywork, a styling cue picked up from the Mustang I. Inside, the GT's five-instrument cluster was anchored in the center by a round 140 mile-per-hour speedometer that replaced the long, horizontal 120 mile-per-hour version of the non GTs.

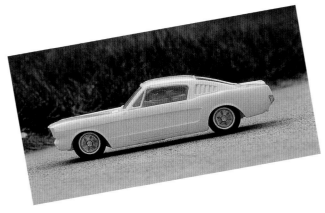

Ford Motor Company and a variety of toymakers around the world began producing Mustang models and toys almost as soon as the cars were introduced. Japanese toymakers especially loved the cars and produced models as police cars, ambulances, and even notchbacks for FBI commanders. Ford's own 1/25th scale promotional models were precise replicas that were given to the children of good customers. This generated the repeat business that saw the children return as adults to buy real Mustangs.

Instead of a separate luxury model, a different set of options, including the Interior Decor group (providing an 8,000 rpm tachometer and a clock on separate pods straddling the steering column and a full-length console), Accent groups, a full-width bench seat with center armrest, air conditioning, a deluxe steering wheel, and even vinyl roof covering, had to suffice for those more interested in getting to the golf course in style than getting around a race course in time.

By now, Jacque Passino and Ford's racing effort was taking back the tracks. Mustangs replaced the Falcon in international competition and two of Ford's hardtops, entered by Alan Mann Racing in England, won the Touring Class of the 1964 Tour de France. This was a brutal, nearly 5,000-mile flog over ten days that included eight hill climbs and a total of twelve hours of flat-out racing spread over eight race courses. The rules allowed no repairs overnight, only during event hours, thereby taking

time from competition. Then Jim Clark drove Colin Chapman's Lotus-Ford to victory and into the winner's circle at the 1965 Indy 500. Shelby's Cobras were teaching Ferrari to be graceful in defeat, and Holman and Moody were showing everyone else that the Blue Oval could very well own the super oval by year's end.

The 1966 model was introduced on September 16, 1965, with very few changes. Five months later, 676 days after Job One, the Rouge plant produced Mustang number 1,000,000. The first five regular Mustangs assembled had all been shipped to eastern Canada for display and sale. The first production car, a Wimbledon White convertible with black interior, had sold

Top left
The GT option picked up the styling and engineering feature of running the exhaust tips through the bodywork that had been introduced with Mustang I three years before. Backup lights were a factory-installed option for $10.47 (or done by the dealer for $10.40). Mustang stylists made good use of sharp creases on front and rear fenders.

Top right
Promotional toys helped build the next generation's interest in Mustang.

Left
This is part of Mustang restorer/historian Bob Perkins' collection of promotional models and memorabilia.

in April 1964 in St. Johns, New Foundland, to an airline pilot. In a ceremony back in Dearborn, airline captain Stanley Tucker exchanged his original convertible, car No. 1, for a new silver convertible, car No. 1,000,001.

Above

In all, Ford produced 559,451 late-1965 Mustangs. Of this, only 5,338 were luxury convertible models. (Ford only produced 7,232 Mustangs with the K-code 289 engine during this time period as well.) Standard convertibles outsold luxury models thirteen to one. But rarer than the luxury models were the 2,111 convertibles sold with bench seats.

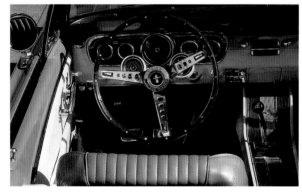

Left

Sport console ($50.41), Rally-Pac (the tachometer and clock mounted on the steering column)($69.30), manual front disc brakes ($56.77), and AM push-button radio ($57.51) all added up. The base convertible sold for $2,557.64. With all these options, this was a $4,000 Mustang.

Styled steel wheels and dual red-line 6.95x14-inch tires were options meant to dress up appearance and improve performance. The wheels were lighter than standard steel wheels, and the tires held the road better. The wheels were available with V-8-powered cars only, for $119.71, while the tires were standard with the K-code engine but cost $48.97 with all others.

5

Spurred on by the Man Called Carroll

Shelby Mustangs 1965–1966

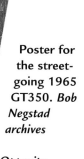

By August 1964, Ford Division management knew that General Motors and Chrysler would not take the Mustang lying down. Rumors drifted over from Warren, the Detroit suburb where General Motor's Technical Center was located, that Chevrolet was hard at work on a challenger to the Mustang that they planned to introduce for 1967. Plymouth's Barracuda was going to be mildly updated for 1966, but for 1967, it would get partially re-skinned and would look much less like the sporty Valiant it had been.

Chevrolet's potent threat to Mustang was the Corvette, which offered a 360 horsepower fuel-injected engine option in 1963 and would have 375 horsepower for 1964. The Stingray styling had created considerable interest, and Ford knew that Corvette's second- and third-year updates would only improve the car's appearance. What was worse, Pontiac had announced a new option for the compact Tempest. It would be called the G.T.O., and it would offer a "tri-power" 389 cubic-inch V-8, fed through three two-barrel carburetors and producing 348 horsepower. In an era of cheap gasoline, these were the first shots fired in the performance war. Mustangs were selling as rapidly as the factories could produce them and the dealers could stock them. But no one at Ford expected this level of sales to last forever.

The broad reach of Ford's "Total Performance" program had taken Mustangs to France and sent Ford engines to California for Carroll Shelby's installation in modified A.C. Ace sports cars. A.C. was nearly out of business when Shelby approached them, but they made a huge comeback because the Cobras captured almost every checkered flag they contested, which in turn captured the hearts and minds of motorjournalists and performance-car fans. A consensus among Ford Division personnel was that it was time to bring some of Shelby's imagination back home.

In a meeting with Lee Iacocca, Shelby learned that Ford had gotten nowhere trying to get the Mustang recognized as a "production race car" for Sports Car Club of America (SCCA) competition in the U.S. But Shelby knew John Bishop, the executive director of the SCCA, and he told Iacocca he believed he knew what it would take to run the pony in Bishop's events.

Bishop told Shelby that to qualify for production classes the car had to be a two-seater and that either the suspension could be modified or the engine could be changed for racing, but not both. The major hurdle was that Shelby would have to have 100 cars manufactured by January 1, 1965, in order to be eligible to race that year. Bishop hinted that he thought this was impossible to accomplish in less than five months. But Bishop didn't know how Ford had been working lately.

Shelby concluded that he could never sell 100 pure race cars. Rick Kopec, editor of the 1987 second edition of the *Shelby American World Registry*, pointed out that Shelby reasoned that he could produce two models, one of them for racing and the other for the street. Racing suspensions were something that Shelby could put a warranty on while racing engines were another matter altogether. Shelby returned to Iacocca and told him that all they needed to do was build a hundred cars and that he knew how to do it. The "Cobra-Mustang" program was approved and launched immediately.

Poster for the street-going 1965 GT350. *Bob Negstad archives*

Opposite
1965 Shelby GT350
Carroll Shelby was a familiar face around Ford Motor Company by the time Ford asked him how to take their new Mustang racing. Shelby learned that the sanctioning bodies wanted to legalize the car for racing and set out to quickly build the first 100 in his shops in Venice, California. The car was originally known as the Cobra-Mustang.

Shelby had a small facility already working in Venice, California, north of Los Angeles International Airport (LAX). In these shops he and his staff produced racing and street Cobras. Ken Miles, an erudite Englishman with a wry wit, was Shelby American's competition director, racer, and development driver. He was given two coupes, some Ford parts books, and sent up to Willow Springs Raceway near Mojave, California. His assignment was to produce a car that would hang onto the race track without becoming undriveable on the street. What's more, it had to be cost effective, modified with parts readily available to keep the final prices reasonable.

With help from Ford chassis engineer Klaus Arning, Miles and Shelby team co-driver Bob Bondurant dialed in the cars and returned to Venice with what became the street Shelby Mustang-Cobra suspension. Near the end of testing, Ford also shipped one of the independent rear-suspension cars out for comparison, but by the time Miles had finished with the first two notchbacks, he had them handling as well as the IRS cars. (This was another factor that contributed to that experimental suspension never seeing production. Shelby and Miles simply said it wasn't necessary.) Shelby then ordered three stock white fastbacks. These San Jose-produced cars became the first prototype street car and the first two race cars. More testing time at Willow Springs sorted these cars out, and Shelby was ready to go to work. Another 100 "knocked down" (the term for incomplete cars) Mustangs were ordered from San Jose. Shelby's cars would leave San Jose as virtually identical, all-white fastbacks with black interiors, equipped with the 271 horsepower 289 cubic-inch engine, 8.75-inch rear ends, and with no hood or latches, grille, radio, seat belts, rear seats, exhaust system, or emblems of any kind.

Aided by Chuck Cantwell, Ford Division's Mustang-Cobra project engineer, other odd parts were found and fitted. One of these was the "export brace," a stiff single piece of stamping that extended from the shock towers to the firewall; this replaced the two-piece braces used on domestic Mustangs and was standard equipment on all Mustangs shipped to Europe. Larger disc brakes and oversize Fairlane station-wagon rear drums were mounted along with an aluminum-

case, Borg-Warner Type T-10, close-ratio four-speed transmission. The 100 cars represented just about two days of production from San Jose—a fact the skeptical Bishop couldn't have known—and as soon as they were completed, they were shipped, six to a carrier, down the coast. Delivery was made not to Shelby's shops in Venice but rather to two huge, leased airplane hangars, part of the former North American Aviation assembly facilities on about twelve-and-a-half acres along the south side of LAX.

Once the cars got to the new shops, the front and rear suspensions were modified substantially. Front upper A-arms were lowered, a chore requiring new locating holes. A 1-inch anti-sway bar replaced the stock 0.625-inch version. The entire rear end—differential and suspension—was removed to cut holes through the floor pan in order to weld brackets in place on which to mount over-ride traction bars. This modification contributed to the handling that matched the IRS car. Koni shocks were used on all four corners. Inside the car, 3-inch wide competition lap belts were bolted through the side frame rails and through the transmission tunnel. The other end of these tunnel bolts held a strap to keep the drive shaft in place. The battery was mounted in the trunk for weight balance. (This was for the first 325 cars only; buyers complained of battery acid fumes corroding the rear deck lid and seeping up into the passenger compartment. From mid-1965 on, the battery was up front.)

Pete Brock (who along with Norm Neumann and Gene Garfinkle had first drawn the mid-engine Corvair-powered Mustang coupe for *Sports Car Graphic* in early 1960) was Carroll Shelby's first employee. Among his accomplishments,

Left
Shelby modified the engines to pull 306 horsepower at 6,000 rpm out of the Ford small-block 289-cubic-inch engine. Torque was 329 foot-pounds at 4,200 rpm. A four-barrel 715 cfm Holley carburetor was fitted onto Shelby's aluminum high-rise intake manifold. Valve covers embossed with the Cobra logo and a larger oil sump, also identified with the Cobra name, were part of the package.

Opposite
Competition versions received a modified, riveted-on, fiberglass front end in place of the front bumper and sheet-metal valence. This served most effectively to funnel air to the oil cooler and to a larger radiator than on Shelby's street cars. This model was built near the middle of the 1965 production run but was used by Shelby for camshaft testing and development and for time trials at the Bonneville salt flats.

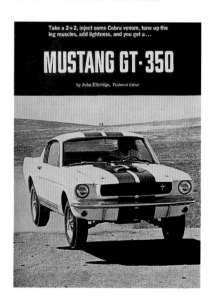

Opening page of the May 1965 issue of *Motor Trend's* review of the Shelby GT350. *Tony Navarra archives. Reprinted by permission, Petersen Publishing*

Koni adjustable shock absorbers were fitted all around, and instead of Ford's usual two-piece shock-tower brace back to the firewall, a single piece, known as the "export brace" was used to stiffen up the front end. The "Monte Carlo" bar, named after the piece used on Falcons for the European rally, tied the two towers together. For better weight distribution, the batteries were mounted in the trunk, although escaping fumes sometimes seeped into the cockpit. After about the 325th car, the battery was moved back up front.

Shelby's modifications to the exterior of the production Mustang were few except for competition versions with their new nose. Most of the effort and money went into making the cars go, stop, and handle. And most of the $4,547 list price went to cover those modifications.

he designed the graphic appearance of the Shelby cars (as well as Shelby's Cobra Daytona coupes). Again, the name issue came back to haunt. Names needed legal approval. Engine designations were fine except that when the engines changed, all the badges and printed material were obsolete. Most race cars—excluding of course Shelby's own Cobra and a few others—went for numbers. The best solution would be to find some designation that didn't mean anything but *seemed* to mean something. A number that suggested more than it revealed. That way, the model could continue for several years, updated constantly, without alerting sanctioning bodies.

The story goes that Shelby looked across the street and asked his chief engineer Phil Remington how far away he thought a building was from where they sat. Guesses were made, and then Remington went out and paced it off. It came to 350 feet. "Fine," Shelby said, "let's call the little car the GT350. If the car's good, the name won't matter, and if it's no good, the name won't matter."

An additional fifteen cars were ordered from San Jose that were to be stripped further than the other 100 cars. These were delivered without side or rear-window glass, interiors, insulation, or head liners, with no heater, defroster, and no gas tank. While work continued at a more accelerated pace on the other 100 cars, these were to be the first race cars. Work went more slowly.

For two years, Shelby had raced the 289 V-8s. His people could charm 385 reliable horsepower out of the Cobra engine, even when somewhat detuned for longer endurance races. For the GT350 race cars, the engines were dismantled, and the heads were sent out in order to have intake and exhaust valve ports enlarged and polished. All of the reciprocating pieces—pistons, connecting rods, crankshafts—were balanced, and the engine was reassembled to "blueprint" tolerances. New specifications called for a high-capacity Holley 715 cfm carburetor that had a center-pivot float. This kept the float from hanging up on one side of its bowl during hard cornering. Tubular steel exhaust headers led to glass-pack mufflers, and most states allowed the exhaust tail pipe to flare out just ahead of the rear tires (except for California and New York, where tail pipes exiting at the rear of the car were mandated). The street engines

produced about 306 horsepower while the racing cars developed between 350 and 360 horsepower in testing on dynamometers.

Race cars weighed some 250 pounds less than the street cars. SCCA rules allowed Shelby to remove front and rear bumpers. The front bumper was replaced with a fiberglass piece with a large lip cut into it to better channel air through an oil cooler and the water radiator. Another hole on either side of the lip led air to the front brakes for cooling. On the side of the fastback roof, the vents were covered to improve airflow. A one-piece fiberglass clip-on hood with functioning air scoop was used for both street and racing models.

When John Bishop's scrutineers showed up at Shelby American shops, they were stunned. Shelby had produced more than his 100 Mustang GT350s. (Some of the race cars were still in preparation.) All of them were parked outside, in clear, tidy rows. In *Competition Press & AutoWeek Magazine*, a story published November 7, 1964, announced that SCCA had homologated the "Mustang-Cobra" for Class B Production racing for 1965. There was no photo of the car, so Corvette racers would only read it and wonder what Shelby had done now.

The first fifteen race cars, known as the GT350 R, were all completed by the spring of 1965. Because Shelby had assembled 100 street models, each with the identical suspension modifications, they became his production base. From that, he could modify his racing engines as much as he pleased. After a track test written by Jerry Titus and published in the March 1965 *Sports Car Graphic*, orders began to arrive. The first two race cars became Shelby American factory entries. The other thirteen were quickly shipped; the first customer car went to Ohio, the second to Ontario, Canada, the third to Switzerland, all in April. Between May and September the rest went all across the U.S. and one to Germany. Shelby meticulously shipped updated information and tips to his customers. He wanted none of the ill-will that he knew existed between other official teams and customers who knew they could never win against the "factory." For Shelby—and for Ford—what was important was that a Mustang won. And win they did. Shelby's GT350 Rs established the same kind of nearly invincible record as

Shelby installed a tachometer and an oil pressure gauge in the notch in the dashboard. While this car was fitted with the competition nose, the interior was pure street car. Racing versions had a simple metal instrument panel and were fitted with competition bucket seats. The fire extinguisher was last inspected in late May 1968.

A corner of the shoulder harness is visible on the roll cage. The spare tire was mounted inside the car in 1965 models for weight balance and to leave some room in an already modest trunk. The standard tire was Goodyear's 7.75-15 Blue Dot.

Ford's standard Fastback 2+2 sold for $2,533.19, the GT package for $165.03, the 271 horsepower 289-cubic-inch engine for another $276.34, and the four-speed transmission for $184.02. With prices this reasonable, it was difficult to option up a high performance 2+2 to cost as much as $4,000. For Shelby to sell his car for $500 more than that but with only two seats struck some buyers as unacceptable. That reaction inspired the more radical-looking Shelby cars that followed.

his Cobras had done in the U.S., Canada, and all across Europe.

For 1966, Shelby withdrew his team from racing. The factory effort had proved its promotional value. Instead, Shelby began paying incentives, and each time a Shelby American Mustang won, its owner got a check for $150; second place was worth $75.

The remaining R-model Mustangs were completed during 1966, twenty in all, and they were given 1966-style grilles even though a number of them were begun in late 1965.

Shelby sold his cars through about eighty-five Ford dealerships. The geographic representation was good, with outlets stretching from Alas-

ka (John Stepp's Friendly Ford on East 5th Avenue in Anchorage) to Florida (J.D. Ball Ford on N.W. 7th Avenue in Miami) and from Maine (Sullivan Ford Sales in Bangor on Hammond Street) to California (in Huntington Beach at Mark Downing Ford on Beach Boulevard). In addition, there was a small number of Shelby American dealers who carried not only the Mustangs but also his 289 and 427 Cobras. He produced a manual for both Ford sales people and his own dealers, complete with an analysis of why Ford's "Total Performance" philosophy was more than just a brief advertising campaign.

"It is a merchandising *platform* for Ford Division . . . one which follows the maxim, 'you can sell an old man a young man's car—but you can't sell a young man an old man's car.'"

The manual outlined who the buyers might be. "Don't overlook the older buyer," it advised, "such as the professional man or executive who may have long been a performance fan but who could not exercise his performance car wishes earlier . . ." It went on to advise that demonstration rides and drives were critical. But risky. "Most motorsport cars demand driver capabilities beyond the average motorist's abilities . . . Caution should be exercised by the sales specialist, especially with a prospect whose answers to performance questions indicate relatively little performance knowledge or who wants to trade up from a 'mild' to 'wild' performance car."

Racing, by the dealership, was encouraged as a way to build dealer name recognition, and from that, to develop a business in new car sales, parts sales, and even to servicing private-owner race cars. Keeping the dealership racing car in the show room or back in the service area where customers could see it—and see the dealer's direct involvement in their sport—would improve traffic into the dealership. Young Motor Company in Charlotte, North Carolina, was quoted: "Whenever we race, the whole town knows the results the next day."

But Shelby presented a realistic approach. Tasca Ford Sales in East Providence, Rhode Island, balanced the enthusiasm. "You must accept the fact that clutches pop, axles break, and engines blow. If you expect these possibilities, if you have money baked into your performance budget to cover them—and if you want to go in spite of them, you'll be okay." Shelby added some shrewd strategy from Al Means Ford in Decatur, Georgia:. "Assisting your own employees with their racing participation is one of the great service department morale builders I know of. The men work on our racing cars strictly on their own time!" And a risk paid off for an Illinois dealer. "One of the smartest things we did last season was to tune a Dodge that actually raced against us. People talked about how it took Ford people to make it run!"

Five pages of sample newspaper ads were included, to make it easier on the new dealers but also to ensure that Shelby American's image looked consistent nationwide. Twelve pages of glossary explained everything from ACCUS (the Automobile Competition Committee for the U.S.) to "four speed" and "glass pack" to "lace" (as in bad rust) and "peel" (as in rubber) and "tuck and roll" and "wild cam." Later pages listed drag classes for stock cars in the National Hot Road Association (NHRA) and American Hot Rod Association (AHRA). Shelby's manual even provided a recommended reading list, including such books as broad in scope as Ken Purdy's *Kings of the Road* and as esoteric as Sir Harry Ricardo's *The High-Speed Internal Combustion Engine*.

Shelby, of course, sold racing engines. Part number S1CR-6003-6 was the 289 Cobra High-Rev Racing Engine, at $3,195 list, $2,445 to the dealer. A competition GT350 road racing engine, part number S1CR-6003-3, was $2,645, $1,995 to his dealers. A carburetor system with a Cobra cast-aluminum manifold and four dual-barrel 48 I.D.A. Weber carburetors along with the necessary pieces to make it work on either the 260 or 289 cubic-inch engines was part number S1CR-9423 at $595, $400 to the dealer. The four-barrel Holley 715 cfm that was standard on GT350 Mustangs, was part number S1MK-9510-A, and dealers charged $87.50 over the counter and paid Shelby $60.90 for it. The plexiglass rear window for the GT350 R models saved between forty and fifty pounds over factory glass. With its 1-inch drop as a vent at the top near the roof, the low-pressure it created exhausted air from the cockpit, and it was supposed to induce a laminar airflow over the rear of the car. This, Shelby claimed, was good for a 5 mile-per-hour top speed increase. It was part number S1MK-40012-A and sold for $137, or $96 to the dealer. Even in those days, it was a very cheap way to give the customer an extra 5 miles per hour.

Finally, Shelby's 120-page manual provided information on taking orders and how delivery would be accomplished—street GT350s were shipped from Los Angeles by rail, while racing Mustangs and all Cobras would come by Shelby American truck—and it spelled out details of the warranty: a period of ninety days or 4,000 miles. "It is understood that any part used in a vehicle for any type of automotive competition, i.e., road racing, drag racing, hill

1966 Shelby GT350H

At airports around the country, Hertz Sports Car Club members could drive away in a Shelby Mustang GT350, complete with automatic transmission and radio. Cars were produced at Shelby's shops at Los Angeles International Airport in hangars that had once belonged to North American Aviation.

One of the most obvious differences between the 1965 GT350 and the 1966 cars was the addition of the rear quarter window cut into the fastback roof. This eliminated a blind spot in rearward visibility that many Mustang owners had complained about. But this was a single-year improvement. The window was clear plexiglass.

A fold-down rear seat was added to the 1966 GT350. Or, more accurately, it was not deleted to make room for the spare tire as had been done with the 1965 model. This was possible also because a rear-suspension modification involving over-ride traction bars for the first year was not carried over.

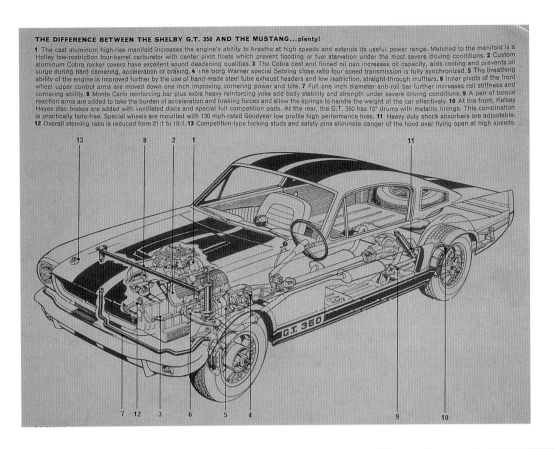

THE DIFFERENCE BETWEEN THE SHELBY G.T. 350 AND THE MUSTANG...plenty!

1 The cast aluminum high-rise manifold increases the engine's ability to breathe at high speeds and extends its useful power range. Matched to the manifold is a Holley low-restriction four-barrel carburetor with center pivot floats which prevent flooding or fuel starvation under the most severe driving conditions. **2** Custom aluminum Cobra rocker covers have excellent sound deadening qualities. **3** The Cobra cast and finned oil pan increases oil capacity, aids cooling and prevents oil surge during hard cornering, acceleration or braking. **4** The Borg Warner special Sebring close ratio four speed transmission is fully synchronized. **5** The breathing ability of the engine is improved further by the use of hand-made steel tube exhaust headers and low restriction, straight-through mufflers. **6** Inner pivots of the front wheel upper control arms are moved down one inch improving cornering power and bite. **7** Full one inch diameter anti-roll bar further increases roll stiffness and cornering ability. **8** Monte Carlo reinforcing bar plus extra heavy reinforcing yoke add body stability and strength under severe driving conditions. **9** A pair of torque reaction arms are added to take the burden of acceleration and braking forces and allow the springs to handle the weight of the car effectively. **10** At the front, Kelsey Hayes disc brakes are added with ventilated discs and special full competition pads. At the rear, the G.T. 350 has 10" drums with metallic linings. This combination is practically fade-free. Special wheels are mounted with 130 mph-rated Goodyear low profile high performance tires. **11** Heavy duty shock absorbers are adjustable. **12** Overall steering ratio is reduced from 21:1 to 19:1. **13** Competition-type locking studs and safety pins eliminate danger of the hood ever flying open at high speeds.

climbs, rallies, etc., shall be excluded from this warranty." No surprise, certainly.

The 1965 racers sold for $5,995 while the street cars sold for $4,547. In 1965, Shelby produced 515 street models, thirty-five competition cars, and nine "drag cars," not including the first three prototypes. As the 1966 model year approached, Shelby looked at what could be done to make his cars different from 1965. He installed a Paxton supercharger on one prototype to evaluate performance differences, and on another car, he fitted the long narrow turn signals taken from the 1965 Thunderbird that lit sequentially. Shelby decided both of these ideas had merit, one near-term, the other for consideration further down the road.

Shelby dealers—meaning Ford dealers—had gotten some feedback from buyers and from potential customers. It was the first time Shelby would hear a litany that would become too familiar over the next several years: the two-seat-only configuration, the limitation of color choice to any so long as it was white, the loud exhaust, loud

rear differential, hard suspension, and any transmission so long as it was the four-speed, floorshift manual. These were comments dealers relayed to Shelby but also to Ford.

To soften the ride, the most time-consuming and costly modifications were eliminated from the 1966 cars. The front upper A-arms were no longer lowered, and the rear end was not cut and changed through the addition of rear over-ride traction bars. (Unfortunately, this negated almost immediately the effects that Ken Miles had accomplished to improve the handling without an IRS option.) When Ford prepared its factories for the model-year changeover, a burst of 252 1965-specification cars was turned out of San Jose, and these were shipped to LAX to become the first of the 1966s. These were white, and as the old saying goes about abused cow ponies, they rode hard and they could be put away wet. After these cars were completed and sold, the rest of the 1966 models were rather kinder and gentler.

For 1966, Shelby sought subtle changes in the street cars. Chuck Mountain at Kar Kraft disliked Ford's functional side vent, and he created a clear plexiglass rear quarter window in place of the vent. Shelby added a functional side scoop to cool the rear brakes. This replaced the nonfunctional decoration on the previous cars for which he had taken some criticism. The battery was permanently installed in the engine compartment, and the spare tire (that had occupied the backseat area—again for weight balance) was put back in the trunk. The rear seat, which may have actually cost Shelby money to have deleted, was restored as a "mandatory option." And an automatic transmission was now available. The color chart was expanded to include Raven Black, Guardsman Blue, Sapphire Blue, Candy Apple Red, or Ivy Green. And Shelby, who had offered the Paxton supercharger as a "parts list" item at $485 complete for owner installation on his 289 Cobras, offered it as a Shelby "factory-only" option for the 289-engined GT350s. (No price was quoted, and it appears that fewer than a dozen 1966 cars were ever delivered with the supercharger.) The cars sold for $4,428, equipped with the automatic or four-speed transmission.

One of the most remarkable offshoots of Shelby's Mustang program came on November

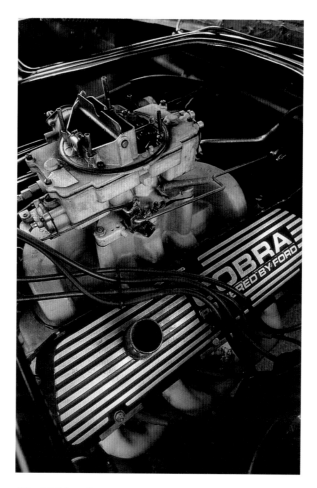

23, 1965, when Hertz Rent-A-Car company ordered 200 GT350s from Shelby American. This order and the 800 cars that followed have made up a huge part of the legacy of the Shelby Mustang. However, it was a story that was straightened out only in the past several years and reported by Greg Kolasa and Carol Padden in the *Shelby American World Registry*.

In 1965, Hertz operated an exclusive program for executive and business travelers who had good credit and clean driving records. This was during a period when Avis was aggressively hounding Hertz for its number one rental car position, and Hertz offered a generous handful of Corvettes to rent to these Hertz Sports Car Club members. Shelby had heard about the club and asked Peyton Cramer, a friend who had arranged the lease of the hangars, to make the initial contact in New York. Before he left, Cramer researched Hertz and learned that John Hertz started out in business in 1925 by buying an existing livery service in Chicago that produced its own

Left
The Shelby-modified 289-cubic-inch engine with its 306 horsepower was unchanged from 1965, save the exhaust system. Exhaust pipes that exited from the body just ahead of the rear tires on 1965 models were straightened out and, ran like regular production cars, out the rear on the 1966-and-later models.

Opposite above
Promotional sales brochure for 1966 Shelby GT350 model. *Tony Navarra archives*

Opposite below
For 1966 the full GT350 production run got functional side scoops just behind the doors to direct air into the rear brakes. In addition, the 1966 cars got backup lights. Shelby provided cars for Hertz Corporation in 1966 and then again in 1968 and 1969, although these later programs were not publicized and the cars were not specially designated with the "H."

Above
The chrome grilles delivered from Ford's plant in San Jose had a flat-black area painted in the center to contrast against the pony logo on regular production cars. Shelby planned to carry over his offset pony and bars, and panic resulted when the new cars arrived. But the paint was easily removed, and Shelby's staff put the pony where they wanted it.

Right top
A dash plaque mounted below the huge tachometer warned drivers about the brakes. "This vehicle is equipped with competition brakes. Heavier than normal pedal pressure may be required." The metallic brake pad material was fade-resistant but did not grab well when the brakes were cold. Routine street driving never gave the brakes time to warm up to racing levels, making the brakes seem insensitive and inadequate.

cars. Hertz's plan was to rent cars for self drive. To promote the livery and the self-drive idea, he had all the cars painted black and yellow-gold. A black-and-gold prototype GT350 was prepared and flown to New York. When Cramer met with Hertz executives, he received a very favorable response. They proposed adding an "H" to the rocker panel tape logo, and after the order was placed, the rental agency began a promotional blitz, announcing the availability of the cars at airports in certain cities. With the ad campaign underway, an additional 800 cars were ordered on December 21.

Each of the 1,000 cars was to be an automatic transmission version—though the first eighty-five were not—and all were to have radios. The final fifteen were delivered by the end of May 1966. The first two hundred were black with gold stripes and, according to Kolaso and Padden's research, because Hertz had not specified differently, the next 230 cars ended up in a mix of the red, green, blue, and white, all with gold stripes. At that point, Hertz did specify. The rest of the cars

were ordered and delivered in black and gold. Interiors were all black, and all the rental cars had rear seats with standard Ford rear seat belts. Hertz charged $17 per day and seventeen cents per mile and made the cars available only to drivers more than twenty-five years old.

As many misconceptions as Kolasa and Padden cleared up, there are nearly as many stories that may be just as unfounded and capricious about Hertz rental Mustangs going to the races *and racing* while they were there. While the Hertz cars had standard Shelby brakes—with metallic linings that worked best when warm but caused some concern to first-time renters on cold days—they had no roll bars. What's more, while the first eighty-five cars were shipped with stick-shift transmissions (and bolt-in roll bars certainly were available), few racers had faith in competing with an automatic transmission (except possibly for those driving Jim Hall's Chaparrals). Still, it added greatly to the legend and mythology of the Shelby Mustangs.

At the end of the 1966 production run, the last sixteen or so Shelby cars assembled were convertibles. Several of these had automatic transmissions, were air-conditioned, and eventually were given by Shelby to individuals who had helped his company and the Mustang GT350 project above and beyond the call of duty. Each was fitted with the black interior, though the exteriors were white, yellow, red, green, blue, and pink—the pink one reportedly done as a gift to Shelby's secretary.

In all, 1,370 regular-production fastbacks were produced in addition to the 1,000 Hertz cars in 1966. Another four drag cars were produced as well as the convertibles. Between the 2,380 cars in 1966 and the 562 manufactured in 1965, there was only one complaint that Carroll Shelby heard the loudest: it was true that his street cars sold for nearly twice as much money as regular-production cars. But some of the people who *didn't* buy one had the nerve to think—out loud—that the GT350 should *look* like it cost twice as much.

Mustang restorer/collector Bob Perkins has built a replica of a late-1960s showroom/high-performance parts sales display in one of his shops in Juneau, Wisconsin.

Remember, this was a rental car. 289 cubic-inches, 306 horsepower. Shelby did nothing to his engines to make them more durable for rental use. He simply used the same technology in them that he used in his very reliable racing versions. But this was a rental car!

Nearly all the Hertz rentals were delivered with automatic transmissions. About eighty-five of the earliest cars were produced with manual gearboxes, but it is a safe guess that clutch replacement quickly ate up any profit to be had from the $17 daily rental fee.

While nearly 80 percent of the Shelby cars produced for Hertz were done in black and gold, cars in the second shipment slipped out of the San Jose plant in a rainbow of Ford exterior colors. Hertz Sports Car Club charged $17 a day and 17 cents per mile to qualified drivers.

6

Looking Into
The Crystal Ball
1967–1968-1/2

Engines were driving Ford by this time. The thin-wall 221 cubic-inch block—the modular V-8 with five-bolt transmission mounting—had been built for the Fairlane. This was a car whose front bay would not accommodate any of the big-block engines even if they could be sleeved in order to reduce displacement and power. Thin-wall casting requires meticulous attention both to designing the block and, more importantly, to pouring the iron in the foundry. Cores placed within the casting to represent cylinders and other essential passages had to be exactly positioned. But the benefit of this precision was a weight savings of as much as one third over the big-block castings.

Maintaining the precise location of the cores in the blocks meant that overboring was then possible. Ford initially enlarged the displacement to 260 cubic-inches and got 164 horsepower out of the same five-bolt block. (This was the first engine Ray Geddes shipped to Shelby in California.) But soon after, the six-bolt 289 cubic-inch version was available, producing 271 horsepower. The "High-Performance 289" became the foundation of the "Powered by Ford" legend. This was quickly delivered to Shelby to replace the 260s in his Cobras. In production dress it became a standard option—known as the famous K-code engine—in the Mustangs. It was also the basis of the power plant for Ford's first GT40 race cars. Shelby, as mentioned earlier, derived 306 horsepower from this engine for the street GT350; he and Ford engineers pulled nearer 390 horsepower from racing Mustangs, Cobras, and early GT40s.

Eventually, with larger bores and longer strokes, the 221 cubic-inch 145 horsepower engine would grow all the way to 351 cubic-inches. This displacement was manufactured—with divergent performance characteristics and goals—in

the Cleveland, Ohio, engine plant and the Windsor, Ontario, plant. First produced in the Windsor engine facility in 1969, it was known as the 351W. But this was not the performance engine. Its destination was primarily light trucks. Sharing its bore, stroke, and overall displacement—but almost nothing else—was the 1970 351C engine, the Cleveland plant high-performance version. The Cleveland version used substantially different cylinder heads to obtain the power that the Windsor engine never sought. While two- and four-barrel carburetors were offered on both engines, the later model 351 HO—high output, introduced out of Cleveland in May 1971 and produced only through 1973—became the engine to look for (or to watch out for if you were driving a 350 V-8 Camaro or a 360 V-8 Plymouth Barracuda or Dodge Challenger).

Ford's other engines were its big-blocks. While the 289 cubic-inch engine was a product of the Fairlane thin-wall 221, the huge 390 cubic-inch V-8 that was offered in the regular production-run 1967 Mustangs was the shot fired in declaration of the horsepower war. The recoil from this potent weapon widened the Mustang. In order for this big engine to fit into the Mustang's engine bay, the car's width spread more than 2-1/2 inches. Front and rear track grew by 2 inches. While this was done partially to accommodate the weight of the 390, it also accomplished better handling for the small-block 289-engined cars. A few of the tricks that Carroll Shelby had employed on his 1965 GT350 had been overruled as too costly to re-appear in 1966. But then, some of these showed up on the Dearborn-, San Jose- and Metuchen-built cars in 1967, hidden from view by

Ford used both photography and artwork in its Mustang brochures and for the rest of its product line as well.
Tony Navarra archives

Opposite
1968 GT390
In 1968, the two-door Fastback was a popular car with about 42,580 sold. Base price was $2,578.60. The GT package was $146.71, four-speed transmission was $233.18, and the S-code 390-cubic-inch engine was $263.71.

1968 GT390

Steve McQueen leapt the streets of San Francisco in one of these. The GT390 that he used in the film Bullitt (two, in fact) was prepared by Los Angeles auto racer Max Balchowski. He fitted koni shocks all around, lowered the car, and used much stiffer springs on the front end in order to survive the hard landings downhill. Balchowski's modifications cost less than $200 and required barely ten days.

the fatter tires. The front-suspension characteristics were revised when the engine compartment was widened to accept the big-block engines. This meant that instead of the front tires seeming to roll under the car while cornering—a condition called camber loss—the tires on the 1967 and later cars remained perpendicular. Improving cornering and handling normally required stiffer springs and larger front anti-sway bars; these additions would cause the ride to stiffen up as well. However, the Shelby- and Fairlane-inspired modifications resulted in benefits in handling *and* ride comfort.

The big blocks, Ford's most effective weapons in the performance wars, ranged from 332 cubic-inches up through the 390 and on to 427 and 428 cubic-inches. (A third series also produced the 429 and 460 cubic-inch blocks as well.) The 390 first appeared in 1961. It was thoroughly developed by the mid-1960s, and it utilized hydraulic cams and a Holley four-barrel carburetor to produce 320 horsepower. It was offered as a $232 option in the 1967 Mustang. For 1968, the engine was renamed the GT390, and it offered five more horsepower.

Back in 1962, Pontiac Division of General Motors staked its claim on NASCAR. Competing with its 427 cubic-inch V-8s, it ran away from Ford's 406s. Ford knew that by enlarging the bore of the big blocks, it could reach 427 cubic-inches as well. In late 1963, Ford offered a 427 in limited quantities for the Galaxy and the Fairlane. Called the Thunderbolt, this was available as a racing engine with one or two four-barrel carburetors mounted on either medium- or high-rise intake manifolds. Ford's efforts paid off. Fairlane "T-bolts" won the NHRA Super Stock category at the 1964 Winternationals.

The 427 soon appeared in Shelby's Cobra, turning an impressive and well-balanced 289-engined sports car into something else again. Race-driving technique for the big-block Cobra was likened to competing in a series of drag races that were interrupted by corners. In Shelby's Cobras and in Ford's GT40s—known at this time as the Mark II 427 GT—a single four-barrel carburetor was used on a medium-rise intake manifold. Tuned to last through an endurance race—from a few hundred miles up to a few thousand (such as at Le Mans or Daytona)—the 427 side-oiler pro-

As the muscle-car war intensified, this was the engine that Ford threw into the fray. This big block forced the widening of the 1967/68 Mustang bodies by 2 inches. The S-code versions, "Thunderbird Special 390," was offered in the Mustang in 1968. With bore and stroke of 4.04x3.78 inches, Holley four-barrel carburetor, and 10.5:1 compression, Ford rated the engine at 325 horsepower at 4800rpm with 427 foot-pounds of torque at 3200rpm. Its flight characteristics can be seen in *Bullitt*.

Left
This was the real office of San Francisco detective Frank Bullitt and countless wannabees. The two actual film cars have disappeared, but several replicas have been created in honor of McQueen's low-altitude flight in a car originally named after a real high flier.

Opposite
Mustang already had a kind of history by the time this car appeared. The first Mustang, introduced in April 1964, set a precedent for mid-model year introductions that Ford Division would honor for years to come. In some cases it made sense; developments sometimes took longer than anticipated. So on April 1, 1968, Ford introduced the 428-cubic-inch Cobra Jet engine. It could only be ordered with the GT package.

Below
1968-1/2 Cobra Jet coupe
Even from the front there are clues to betray the high-performance nature of this coupe. Hood lock-pins. A ram-air induction scoop. A deep oil sump flanked by dual exhaust pipes. Fat tires. This is no commuter car.

duced a reliable 485 horsepower on 82-octane French gasoline. This was the engine that fulfilled Henry Ford II's dream to win Le Mans. He did it first in 1966 and then repeated from 1967 through 1969.

In 1968, Ford introduced a hydraulic-lifter version of the 427 for the street. (Two years earlier, Ford had introduced the 428, also derived from the 390. This was a performance option for the Galaxies only in the fastback. Using hydraulic cams, the 428 was developed as a lower-cost alternative to the technically more sophisticated, mechanical-cam 427 engines. This was quickly seen as beneficial to the Mustang and to its cousin, the newborn Mercury Cougar, as well as to the Ford Fairlane and Mercury Comet.)

Anthony Young, in his book, *Ford Hi-Po V-8 Muscle Cars*, reported that Bob Tasca, the Providence, Rhode Island, Ford and Shelby dealer, ob-

tained some police interceptor 428s early in 1967. Tasca began to modify and install them in Mustangs for drag racing. Carroll Shelby had received some early engines and with them he developed the GT500KR—the King-of-the-Road package—for street use with this new engine. Ford Division, Young reported, had been searching for a name for its new performance engine; somehow, someone imaginatively merged a Shelby name with another airplane name. A new performance icon was christened: the 428 Cobra Jet.

Conspiring to benefit from all of this enthusiasm for high-powered engines and high-performance automobiles was a bit of skullduggery going on in downtown Detroit at General Motors' corporate headquarters. There is an old adage in business: Hell hath no fury like an executive scorned. On February 6, 1968, the furies arrived at Ford World Headquarters and moved into the President's office in the person of Semon E. Knudsen. "Bunkie," as he was known, had been passed over for the presidency of General Motors, and Henry Ford II picked up the displaced executive. Knudsen was an innovative car enthusiast, energetic and product-oriented, and in his time at GM, he had encouraged the creation of the Camaro and its Trans-Am race-series-inspired derivative, the Z/28. He had vigorously pushed Pontiac Division's GTO and other John DeLorean-directed inspirations. Now Knudsen, who knew GM's plans for a few years down the road, unleashed the furies of Hell on his former employer.

To Knudsen this meant getting as much good-looking, fine-handling Ford horsepower into the marketplace as quickly as possible. He soon learned that he was preaching to the converted. A number of projects already were underway that were meant to pursue exactly that goal.

By the time all the necessary engine testing and chassis development was completed, the 428 Cobra Jet Mustang was ready for introduction as a 1968-1/2 model, barely a few months after Knudsen's arrival. This engine essentially replaced the small production run made of the 427 cubic-inch engine equipped with low-rise intake manifolds, and rated at a more impressive 390 horsepower. As a $622 option, the W-code engine was a rare and lusty handful.

The Cobra Jet was a somewhat better bargain—at $434—but buyers reading the catalogs believed Ford had gone absolutely the wrong direction. With a single 735cfm four-barrel Holley carburetor, Ford rated its output at 335 horsepower. Buyers and drivers quickly learned how conservative this number was. *Hot Rod* magazine tested a 428CJ in a Mustang fastback and achieved 0–60 mile-per-hour times of 5.9 seconds, and standing start quarter-mile runs at 106.6 miles per hour in 13.56 seconds. Actual horsepower was at least 400.

It was available only in the GT package, and it was delivered with a functional, ram-air, cold-air induction hood scoop and power front disc brakes. The car could be ordered with either an automatic three-speed transmission or a four-speed manual. While 654 notchbacks were assembled, 2,253 fastbacks were made and a handful of convertibles were produced as well. To keep it on the road, Goodyear introduced its wider F70 Polyglas tires for the Cobra Jet.

Observers blessed with 20/20 hindsight have complained that the 1967 Mustang got too big and too heavy; that it grew too much too quickly. At the time that its appearance was being planned, people like Gene Bordinat, Don Frey, Hal Sperlich, and so many others each looked into their own crystal ball. But all they saw was fog.

Designs for the 1967 body were begun just as the 1964-1/2 cars were being readied for introduction. No one knew what public response was going to be. Iacocca had his hopes, just as Dave Ash, Bob Negstad, Hal Sperlich, and so many others did. But no one knew. The American car-buying public was a hard audience to play to. The Detroit automakers had gotten into a habit that had spoiled their customers. Every three years they introduced a new body style. With development turnaround time running between three and four years, this practice had cast stylists and engineers alike into the roles of visionaries.

The public had gone wild over the 1955 Thunderbird, and Ford sold 16,000 of them. The same public went even more wild over the 1958 four-seater, and Ford sold more than 40,000 of them despite its mid-year introduction. This same "public"—and especially the automotive journalists—went crazy over Mustang I. Then eighteen months later the "public"—and particularly the automotive journalists—went nuts over the production notchback coupe and convertible.

What was a product planner to do? Where was a stylist to find the answers? Which influences could an engineer trust?

The only thing that seemed certain in late 1964 was that horsepower would become a significant factor in car sales to the audience to whom Ford had directed its Mustang. Big power from Ford at that moment meant the big Thunderbird 390. That engine was simply too large to fit between the wheel wells of the 1965 and 1966 cars. Mustang buyers were fortunate that the people in charge were individuals sensitive to proportion; as the car grew 2 inches in width and length, nothing bulged or bubbled awkwardly.

The risk of bad design was there. Engine and powertrain considerations strained the package

again when, for 1969 and 1970, 427, 428 and 429 cubic-inch engines were offered. Ironically, it was during the period when engine sizes were contracting that the next body design literally would represent a stretch of the envelope.

Left
Cars equipped like this always trigger hundreds of questions decades later. There is no tachometer, but there is an AM radio. There is an automatic transmission and a vinyl roof. It had power steering, power front disc brakes, and a limited slip differential. Who would have ordered something civilized enough to not look out of place at the office, the market, the country club, or Sunday morning church services, yet stuffed with a drag racer's engine?

Next pages
Goodyear Polyglas F70-14 tires were introduced for the 428CJ package. Only 564 hardtops (notchbacks) were produced. The hardtop was base priced at $2,578.60, and the CJ engine was a $434.00 option. The automatic transmission was another $233.17, and the GT package remained $146.71. The vinyl roof set the owner back another $74.36.

GET A KNOCKOUT OF A DEAL NOW...

...on the original and still lowest-priced sports car with bucket seats!

MUSTANG HARDTOP There's no extra cost for bucket seats, floor-mounted stick shift and wall-to-wall carpeting...and you can get the big 390 cu. inch V-8 engine and stereo tape deck as options on all three rakish Mustang models!

Haidlen FORD-MERCURY
1355 EAST F ST.   P. O. BOX 516
OAKDALE, CALIFORNIA   95361

Above
Ford's sales brochure for the 1967 Mustang promoted its new 390-cubic-inch V-8 engine and the "Stereosonic" tape system.
Tony Navarra archives

Right
1968 GT/California Special
The GT/California Special grew out of an idea Carroll Shelby had. Lee Grey, Ford district sales manager for southern California saw it in August 1967. He liked its styling and got it to Dearborn to show Lee Iacocca. Production was approved as a California-only car, and it was introduced February 15, 1968.

Opposite top right

The 302-cubic-inch V-8 replaced Ford's tried-and-true 289 by mid-1968. The standard Autolite four-barrel carburetor in concert with 10.0:1 compression, provided 230 horsepower at 4,800 rpm and 310 foot-pounds torque at 2,800 rpm. In the late 1960s, Ford and Shelby performance parts were sold over the counter in Ford dealerships, and owners often enhanced engine performance as much as their wallets would bear.

Left

Its appearance reflects some of the subtlety Carroll Shelby advocated in his Mustang's early days. The GT grille bars were deleted as was the pony, and the small, round fog lights were replaced with Marchal (later with Lucas) driving lights. The GT/CS package was a $194.31 option, which did not include the $146.71 GT package. In fact, it appears that fewer than 8 percent of GT/CS cars were also GTs.

Top
Automatic transmission, tilt-away steering wheel, and AM/FM stereo radio dressed up the interior. The California Special package did little to the interiors but was limited to exterior dress-up that included the tail spoiler, nonfunctional side scoops, side stripes, and quarter-twist hood locks.

Bottom
Following the mid-February introduction, Ford's Shelby-producer A.O. Smith Corporation manufactured about 4,325 California Specials at its Ionia, Michigan, shops. But the cars did not remain exclusive to California. The Denver area dealers succeeded in getting their own version out of that production run as well. It was called the High Country Special.

Opposite top
When Carroll Shelby first proposed mounting a Paxton supercharger on Ford's 428 Cobra Jet, he installed the prototype engine in a hardtop notchback bedecked with spoilers and scoops that he painted red. Known as *Little Red,* it was trotted out to Ford executives as well as magazine writers to test the market interest. The engine package was never offered, but the body styling became the GT/CS.

Below right
Following its astonishing performance in the 1964 Tour de France, Ford's Mustang became a very popular car throughout France and the rest of Europe. Ford of France distributed full car-line brochures. *Gary Hansen archives*

7

Moving Venice to Michigan
Shelby Mustangs 1967–1968

All the while that Carroll Shelby was involved with his GT350s, he had divided his time unequally between Los Angeles and Slough, England, where Ford Advanced Vehicles was building its GT40 race cars. Ford Division's primary racing and promotional thrust was now in international competition. Henry Ford II had made it clear: his goal was to win the 24 Hours of Le Mans and to beat Ferrari. He wanted to do this not only in a car "powered by Ford" but in a car *called* a Ford. Depending on where Shelby was needed most, he flew between England and California with the frequency and regularity of the tides.

In 1964, Shelby's Cobra coupe had placed fourth overall and first in the GT class at Le Mans, although neither of the two GT40s had finished the race. All the GT40s and the Cobras broke in 1965. So in 1966, an all-out effort resulted from the previous embarrassment. It paid off. Ford GT Mk IIs took first, second, and third. Henry Ford II's goal for 1967 was to make it clear that 1966 was no fluke.

Shelby got photographs of the 1967 production Mustang and then got a set of dimensions. The car had grown, and some of the factory changes in design and chassis would make it difficult to modify for B production racing. What's more, he had ended production of his 427 cubic-inch engine Cobras, and a number of both racing and street versions remained unsold, parked behind the hangars in Los Angeles. With his growing commitment to the GT40 program, competing in 427 Cobras and GT350 R Mustangs clearly was going to be left to Shelby customers.

Significantly, Ford did offer Shelby the big-block 428 cubic-inch Cobra Jet engine for the Mustang, and in some limited cases, even the 427 cubic-inch engines were available. Shelby re-named the engine the Cobra Le Mans, and while plans for utilizing these engines were in the works, he must have looked out the window once again. He probably wondered how much further the old building across the street from his Venice shops was, now that he had relocated to the south side of L.A. airport. He came up with the designation GT500 for the 1967 big-block Cobra Jet versions of his Mustang.

When Ford product planners suggested to him that he put his effort and investment towards the outside of his Mustangs rather than under the hood and underneath the cars as he had done with the 1965 and 1966 models, he did not argue. Producing thousands of cars a year was big business, and it had begun to wear on Shelby who, more and more, missed the pure pleasure of solving racing problems.

According to Wally Wyss in his 1979 book *Shelby's Wildlife*, Ford stylist Chuck McHose was loaned to Shelby from Dearborn. He arrived in advance of the pre-production prototype 1967 body that Ford Division had sent out so that Shelby American could do its own appearance, chassis, and engine modifications. McHose worked with Pete Stacey and Shelby's in-house designer Pete Brock. Together they created the things that would make the GT350 and GT500 look like they *were* worth more money than the regular production fastbacks. They lengthened the hood 3 inches and recessed the grille deeper into the cavity in front of the radiator. Stacey came up with the idea

One-sheet handout promotional flyer for 1967 Shelby GT350 and GT500 Mustang. *Tony Navarra archives*

Opposite
1968-1/2 GT500 KR
Shelby always stretched the performance and styling envelopes. His 1968-1/2 GT500KR was no exception. As he had with his center-located headlights on his early 1967s, he used driving lights in the grille area on the King of the Road and installed a rollover bar on his coupes and convertibles and managed to make these important functional improvements stylish, appealing, and desirable.

The 1967 GT350 and its big brother the GT500 were the last Shelbys produced directly by Shelby at his Los Angeles International Airport shops. Beginning with 1968 production, the assembly was handled by A.O. Smith Company at one of their facilities in Livonia, Michigan. There were other differences, too, that made the 1967s the last pure Shelby Mustangs.

of the headlight high beams mounted in the center of the grille.

A huge scoop was integrated more completely into the hood design than had been done for the 1965 and 1966 models, and side scoops resembling those of the GT40s were added to the sail area on the side of the roof behind the doors. Taking a cue from the GT40s, some of the early 1967 Shelbys had small red marker lights mounted in the side roof vent exits. Endurance racers mounted lights on their cars' sides or roof to illuminate the racing numbers. Sometimes the crews

individually color-coded these lights and the race cars for easier recognition at night by timing and scoring personnel.

Aside from the center-mounted headlights, the next most notable feature was the large, rear spoiler added to the Shelby GTs. Ford's 1967 design had extended the roof line to the end of the body. The Shelby spoiler was reminiscent of the tail on the Cobra coupes that Pete Brock had designed. So these were adapted and set on a steep angle over the Mustang taillight valence. The Thunderbird sequential taillights that had been tried on a 1966 prototype were adopted now, taken from Cougar's parts bins, this time for use in the new cars. These added to the stronger visual identity of the 1967 Shelbys.

The Mustang suspension was reworked once more, primarily to further soften the ride. Buyers who had believed they wanted a race car became less certain once they owned a 1965 or 1966 street GT350. Front anti-sway bar diameter was reduced very slightly, but it was still thicker than what came from Ford in the heavy-duty suspension option. Shelby still used his own variable-rate springs. However, some of the suspension modification was done in order to reduce production costs. Gabriel adjustable shocks replaced the more expensive Koni adjustables imported from Holland.

The 1967 GT350 used the same solid valve-lifter, 289 cubic-inch, 306 horsepower engine that had appeared in the 1965 and 1966 models, still with the cast-aluminum, high-rise intake manifold with the 715 cfm Holley sitting on top. However, federal emissions regulations took away the steel-tube headers. The 428CJ was to be rated at 335 horsepower; this extremely conservative figure resulted as much from efforts to sneak the engine into a lower class of NHRA drag racing as to deflect growing concerns over performance versus safety that were voiced by the insurance industry. For Shelby's adaptation, the 428 was fitted with two Holley 650 cfm four-barrel carburetors mounted on a medium-rise intake manifold. Hydraulic lifters quieted engine noise for the customers who wanted a race car without the noise and harshness of a *real* race car.

The biggest problem for 1967 was that the Mustang grew not only in dimensions but also in weight. Lee Iacocca's first 2,500-pound coupe had grown to about 2,800 pounds as Shelby's 1966 GT350 and would be about 2,750 pounds in the 1967 model. The 428-engined GT500 weighed 3,286 pounds and while the extra 49 horsepower pretty nearly made up for the extra 500 pounds of weight, nothing compensated for the weight bias that now was skewed to the front: 57.4 percent versus 42.6 percent in the rear (the '67 GT350 was 53/47). Fuel economy—something barely even considered in 1967—was another gripe that would be registered against the

GT500. The eight-barrel Cobra Jet was good for 6 to 11 miles per gallon, depending on which magazine tested it (*Sports Car Graphic* got 9.4 miles per gallon); the GT350 still would squeeze out 15 miles per gallon if it was judiciously driven. Base price of the GT350 was reduced once more, to $4,195, and for the GT500, the buyer paid $4,395, although few of either of the models were ever delivered without additional options.

Car & Driver magazine put in context the 1965 and 1966 289-engined Mustangs when it first tested the GT500 for its February 1967 issue.

"The GT500 is an adult sports car. The '65 GT350 was a hot-rodder's idea of a sports car—a rough-riding bronco that was as exciting to drive as a Maserati 300S, and about as marketable a

Above
The California Department of Motor Vehicles looked at red marker lights high up on the side of passenger cars produced by Carroll Shelby and Ford Motor Company and went through the roof. Only emergency vehicles were allowed to wear red lights on the side. Only those roughly 200 GT350 and GT500 cars already produced were able to keep the lights.

Left
As much as the California Department of Motor Vehicles disliked the red marker lights on the side of the roof, it cared no more for Shelby's bright-beam headlights mounted along the car's center line. The State overruled Shelby; which eventually proved beneficial. The headlights blocked airflow to the radiator which improved with their relocation to the more traditional position.

Shelby's postcard announced the arrival of the 1967 GT500. This was an early card showing an early car, complete with center-mounted bright headlights and red marker lights on the roof. *Tony Navarra archives*

proposition. The traction bars clanked, the side exhausts were deafening, the clutch was better than an advanced Charles Atlas program, and when the ratcheting-type limited-slip differential unlocked, it sounded like the rear axle had cracked in half. It rode like a Conestoga wagon and steered like a 1936 Reo coal truck—and we loved it.

"Jumping into the GT500," the reviewer continued, "the most marked difference was in engine noise, which is practically nonexistent in the 428-engined car except for a motorboating throb . . . All the viciousness had gone out of the car, without any lessening of its animal vitality. It still reacts positively, but to a much lighter touch."

While Shelby had taken much of the race car skittishness and sensitivity out of the new cars, he put in a pair of features that restored the sensation of race cars. Shelby installed a roll bar in the fastbacks, welded to the floor pan, and he attached to those roll bars a pair of inertia-reel-fed shoulder harnesses that could be used along with the standard Ford lap belt. (At this time, Federal

safety regulations required over-the-shoulder-across-the-chest clip-in belts, but Shelby deleted these to add the vertical belts that split behind the driver or front-seat passenger's neck and attached at the sides of the seat. This system did make rear-seat entry more of a challenge, however.) Air conditioning as well as automatic transmissions were options ordered more and more often. Buyers were beginning to reflect Ford management's thinking of ten and fifteen years before: shifting gears was something they had already done, now they'd let the car do it.

As production increased, Ford Division offered Shelby a specialist who could help if glitches occurred. Fred Goodell arrived at the hangars and found nothing like Ford production-line efficiency. The 1967 prototype shipped to Shelby American had apparently suffered some chassis torsional twisting in earlier development work. While McHose, Stacey, and Brock carefully designed the fiberglass body pieces according to the plans that Ford shipped, each prototype piece was test-fitted onto the car body. Then production was ordered. The result was that many of these pieces didn't fit the San Jose production bodies and immense amounts of sanding were required to fair them into the production cars. The sanding was done by hand.

David Mathews and Rick Kopec reported in the *Shelby American World Registry* on the comedy of errors that occurred when Goodell arrived just after the twentieth car was complete. No one at Shelby had bothered to clear any of the styling changes with any state regulatory agencies. But there were other problems to solve and by the time Goodell got up to Sacramento, California, the first stop on his mission, about 200 cars had been built. He learned that California—and indeed many other states—had prescribed minimum distances allowed between headlights. And the only vehicles that could operate with red marker lights

on their sides were emergency vehicles, such as ambulances and fire trucks. California thought Shelby was just a division of Ford, not an independent, and they felt Ford was trying to circumvent laws through Shelby.

Their answers? No. And no. Spread out the brights and remove the red lights.

Near the end of 1967 production and as Shelby American was gearing up for the 1968 car run, the lease on the old North American Aviation hangars on Imperial Highway expired. Another airport-related business wanted the space, and zoning regulations gave it priority. Shelby had to move. It proved to be a blessing for him. His production had increased for 1967, and even with his two huge hangars, he didn't have enough room. Ford Division saw the situation as an opportunity to bring under tighter control some of the situations that had caused problems with the California Department of Motor Vehicles (among others). It also knew that it could produce Shelby's cars closer to home more efficiently (with some of the work done as part of its regular assembly-line

process) and thereby save the costs of freight that were added to each car. Production was relocated to facilities operated by an experienced car-assembly subcontractor, A.O. Smith in Ionia, Michigan. Ford was effectively taking assembly—and quality control—supervision "in house." Shelby used his new-found freedom to concentrate on fulfilling Ford's new efforts in the Trans-Am series, having accomplished Henry Ford II's goal of a second win at Le Mans.

The GT350 suffered some in 1968, losing its legendary, noisy, mechanical valve-lifter, 289 cubic-inch engine to "progress" in the form of a quieter hydraulic-lifter 302. The 715 cfm Holley four barrel from the 1967 Shelby was replaced as well, with a 600 cfm Holley, a unit more comfortable with the lower-speed engine. Still for those who craved the additional power, the Paxton-McCullough supercharger option was still available, boosting the 302 from 250 horsepower at 4,800 rpm to 335 horsepower at 5,200 rpm.

Stylistically for 1968, Shelby's band of merry car makers changed the headlights back to big singles and installed Lucas driving lights in the grille. They elongated the hood's overbite even farther and widened the twin air-scoop nostrils making the entire front end look like a road shark in need of feeding. In addition to the 302-powered GT350s, the 427—now quieted by using hydraulic lifters and fitted with the Holley 600 cfm carburetor to deliver 400 horsepower at 5,600rpm—was available for the GT500. However, dealers did their best to talk buyers out of it and reportedly fewer than fifty were produced. To replace that engine, Shelby advertising before the new model year announced the introduction of a 428 cubic-inch engine option with as much as 390 horsepower. This was the earlier 428 cubic-inch version, but updated with new cylinder heads that provided much larger intake and exhaust ports. For the Shelbys, this "police-interceptor" engine used the Holley 715 cfm carburetors.

The hairiest incarnation of the GT500 was named the King of the Road and boasted the 335 horsepower Cobra Jet engine, special side-tape markings, and a large Cobra on each front fender. Unfortunately for enthusiasts hungry for performance, the introduction of this ground-pounder

Shelby adopted many race-car features to his "production" cars. Among them were the controversial roof lights. Endurance racers used marker lights in odd places so their pit crews and timing personnel could spot the cars at night. It was distinctive, and along with the roll bar and air scoops, it was very much in the tradition of road racing.

was postponed by two specific causes. First, a labor strike delayed production of many Ford products at the beginning of the model year. Second, the U.S. Environmental Protection Agency (EPA) emission standards testing and certification took longer than expected, and that slowed the KR to 1968-1/2 introduction. (A planned supercharged Cobra Jet was a victim of emissions testing standards. It was first shown in a Shelby notchback that became the GT/California Special.)

The GT500 KR 2+2 used the 428CJ. However, to the purists the car had come to reflect more Ford and less of the magician from Venice.

"Carroll Shelby might not be a prisoner in the Ford works," wrote *Car Life* magazine's reviewer in its not wholly enthusiastic October 1968 evaluation of the car, "but every year the Shelby Mustang is a little less Shelby, and a little more Mustang. The first Shelbys, still competitive in road racing and as sports cars at that, were thoroughly revised, with improved front suspension geometry and trailing arms to change and limit movement of the live rear axle. Maybe it wasn't necessary, maybe the customers wouldn't pay for something that didn't show. But now, as mentioned, the Shelby version is Mustang, stiffened."

Steve Kelly, in the November 1968 *Hot Rod*, expressed similarly guarded enthusiasm. His comments pointed out how, for an automaker, succeeding at eliminating some customer's complaints evoked others' dissatisfaction.

"Had it not been for Carroll Shelby's 1965-66

"'65-'66 machines..."

Performance was better than "deluxe," but, of course, Shelby had spoiled his enthusiasts and reviewers in the past. *Hot Rod*, testing the 3,570 pound, $4,857 fastback, could achieve no quicker times than 14.01 seconds in the quarter-mile, crossing the line at 102.73 miles per hour. A roll-bar equipped convertible—heavier by 170 pounds and more costly by $500—could only do 97.71 miles per hour in 14.58 seconds.

"They are now much quieter," Kelly

Opposite below
1968-1/2 GT500KR
It's hard to know whether it's a trick of the eye or a trick of smart psychology. Nearly every Mustang—sitting at rest—looks to be under acceleration, getting going, moving out. Even perfect restorations sit back on their haunches, inviting a hard run up through the gears.

Top
The GT500 name came—legend has it—from Shelby's desire to have a number on the side of his car that was bigger than anyone else's. Chrysler had 426s and 440s, GM had 427s and 454s. Not even Ford was exempt with its 428, 429, and 460. So Shelby had 500.

Left
An optional feature on 1968 Ford products was the swing-away steering wheel to provide easier entry and exit. It always gave the appearance, however, of a broken steering column. And an interlock—among the first of the theft protection safety features—prevented starting with the wheel up.

series GT350 with its worthwhile features as a sports and performance machine, Ford probably wouldn't be marketing the current breed of GT350s and GT500s. Nor is it likely that such a car would've developed," Kelly wrote. "Who knows, FoMoCo may not even *like* perpetuating the brand, but they are, and with greater success than when control was in Shelby's hands. Now the cars are made in Ionia, Michigan, feature bigger power plants, and more closely approach the deluxe appointments of Chevy's Corvette, although lacking the almost complete chassis revision given to the

added, "and have much more distinctive bodies than before. Although this last item doesn't contribute a great deal to the GT's sports car value, it does separate [it] appearance-wise from the regular Mustang. When you're marketing a car, this sometimes is more of a sales tool than ultra-strong and competition-like underpinnings."

Damned if he did, was Carroll Shelby. And damned if he didn't.

Advertisement in 1969 for hair
care products appealed to
Mustang enthusiasts. *Tony
Navarra archives*

The "King of the Road" was Shelby's model name for the 428-cubic-inch Cobra Jet Ram-Air engine. With 335 horsepower on tap at 5,200 rpm, the KR-CJ was good for a quarter-mile in 14.57 seconds at 99.56 miles per hour and 0 to 60 mile per hour times of 6.9 seconds. Not bad performance at all for a car weighing nearly 4,000 pounds.

Left
Carroll Shelby's resident in-house artist Pete Brock and Ford Division's Chuck McHose created the strong visual elements that soon clearly distinguished Shelby's Mustangs from Ford's. The rear deck lid incorporated a large spoiler while McHose and Brock transplanted Mercury Cougar tail lamps to the Mustang's rear.

8

The Pony on Steroids
1969–1970

Farther down the Total Performance engine-displacement spectrum but no less impressive in their performances, Mustangs "Powered by Ford" were competing in the Sports Car Club of America (SCCA) Trans-Am Challenge. This was a road-racing series that—like NASCAR ovals and NHRA drag-racing Super Stock classes—was based on production automobiles. However, the FIA (Federation Internationale de l'Automobile) ruling organization set a sedan class engine displacement limit of 5.0 liters (305 cubic-inches). For Ford, that signaled its 302 cubic-inch V-8. With this engine, heavily developed and strengthened, Ford won the Trans-Am series championship in 1966, its first season, and again in 1967, racing with Shelby American-entered, blue fastbacks. But Chevrolet was challenging Ford by the end of the 1967 season with its new Camaro, and, worried, Ford began to develop a new engine for the 1968 season. But as Ford's new "tunnel-port" 302 became unreliable, Chevrolet got its Z-28 dialed in, and GM's bow-tie division won the title in 1968 and 1969. In 1970, with the racing effort back in control, Ford reclaimed the championship, relying on the formidable driving talents of Californians Parnelli Jones and George Follmer.

With many GT40 engine parts used in the 302 racing blocks, Ford developed up to 400 horsepower—albeit it at very high rpms!—for the Trans-Am series cars. This engine speed and power output was reduced—rated at 290 horsepower at 5,800 rpm but actually producing closer to 310 horsepower in an engine that could be wound up to 7,000 rpm—for the production cars. The street 302 engine also adopted many of the technologies that were invented and proven in the first 289 Hi-Po-based engines for the GT40s as well.

As much as engines played a roll in the success of the car, its handling also won it rave reviews from journalists and owners. In Donald Farr's 1983 book, *Mustang Boss 302: Ford's Trans-Am Pony Car*, Farr quoted Knudsen's philosophy that he carried over from General Motors.

"If a car looks like it's going fast and it doesn't go fast, people get turned off," Knudsen said. "I think if you have a performance car and it looks like a pretty sleek automobile, then you should give the sports-minded fellow—the car buff—the opportunity to buy a high-performance automobile." But the philosophy extended beyond just looks and engines. When the idea to market a street version of the Trans-Am 302 race car took shape, Knudsen set his goal unmistakably. Make it, Farr reported, "absolutely the best handling street car available on the American market!"

The assignment descended from Knudsen to the chief of Light Car Engineering Howard Freers, who gave it to Matt Donner, as principal ride and handling engineer. Donner had been involved with Mustang chassis since the first production cars, and this was an opportunity for him to take the car farther than any production-based Ford had ever gone.

By the time Donner finished with the car, he'd solved a collection of unanticipated problems that all arose trying to make Knudsen's performance Mustang into a Camaro-killer. In some instances it was shades of the '64-1/2 Mustang all over again. The biggest problems arose adapting fat tires to the package. The new F60 Polyglas tires were so stiff that when the car was put through its durability tests, it literally broke the front shock absorber towers. This required significant strength-

The Drag Pack option provided forged connecting rods and a different camshaft inside the 428-cubic-inch V-8. Compression was 10.6:1 and bore and stroke was 4.13x3.98 inches. With a single four-barrel Holley, the engine was rated—for the purposes of lower classification in NHRA competition—at 335 horsepower at 5,200 rpm while torque was rated at 440 foot-pounds at 3,400 rpm. In fact, Ford engineers figured true horsepower was closer to its torque figure than its rated horses.

Left
1970 Drag Pack
The United States was made for cars like this. When county roads were laid out, the map makers gridded much of the country in one-mile squares, and local law enforcement put a stop sign or stoplight at each intersection. For young performance enthusiasts, life could get no better: There was another race track every mile.

ening and modification in structure that had to be done not only to Knudsen's performance 302-equipped cars but to *all* Mustangs. As Howard Freers explained in Gary Witzenburg's *Mustang*, "We had to go back at the last minute and put some rather sizable reinforcements into the vehicle . . . across the board because you can't schedule structural changes for just a certain amount of the cars being built."

The car's appearance was taken care of by another GM transplant, stylist Larry Shinoda whom Knudsen hired away from the Technical Center soon after he arrived at Ford. Shinoda had done several striking GM show cars and had also invented the Camaro rear spoiler and reversed hood scoop. His quick eye caught the graphic treatment on the side of the Ford GT40 Mk IV and adapted it to the race cars and street cars. However, his even greater accomplishment with the 302 was the car's name. Product planners had proposed calling the Trans-Am series street cars the "Trans-Am," but both Knudsen and Shinoda knew Pontiac Division had already protected that name. More than that, the word "boss" had taken on a connotation among young people at and just below the age of the audience to whom this car was aimed. On the street, "boss" meant something undeniably good, and something that was unquestionably at the top of what was available. What's more, Shinoda had always referred to Knudsen as "Boss," and there was nothing wrong with honoring the boss.

The Boss didn't stop at 302. The biggest, baddest Boss was in the works at the same time Matt Donner was trying to tame the handling of the Boss 302. If the Boss 302 was meant to humble the Z/28 on the street and on the road circuit, this car, the Boss 429, was meant to humiliate Chrysler's 426 cubic-inch, 425 horsepower hemi and the rare and exotic Central Office Purchase Order (COPO), cast-iron Mk IV 427 cubic-inch, 425 horsepower Camaros.

As the SCCA's Trans-Am racing series had been birth mother to the Boss 302, so NASCAR was parent of the Boss 429. While Ford's "tunnel-port" 427 cubic-inch engines had been doing well enough on the Super Oval series, the 429 was envisioned as the more powerful successor due to its hemispherical—or nearly hemispherical—

cylinder heads. Chrysler had introduced its Hemi-head engines in the late 1950s for NASCAR and USAC events and in limited production for the street in order to legalize them for racing. Ford's power-plant engineers knew that the domed head is the most efficient combustion chamber form because it leaves no hiding place for the fuel mixture to remain unburned.

In actuality, Ford's 429 was a semi-hemi. The areas of the cylinder head where the valves are located are round in a hemi but flat in a semi-hemi (or crescent shaped in Ford's case). NASCAR required minimum production numbers of any engine to qualify it for racing. So Ford offered the 429 in the Boss Mustang beginning in 1969. The street and race engines, however, were almost completely different.

The first 279 Boss 429 street engines were built with hydraulic lifters and cam. Sometime in mid-1969, Ford changed the engine to use a mechanical cam. The Boss engines, rated conservatively at 375 horsepower, were assembled in the Lima, Ohio, engine facility, but when they were completed, they did not go to Ford's giant Dearborn Assembly Plant (DAP). In fact, car production became quite complex. Engines left Lima and went to Kar Kraft, a kind of official/unofficial Ford shop.

Kar Kraft came from within Ford to establish its unique position outside of Ford. Its pedigree was polished by experience. Roy Lunn, chief of the Mustang I project, who had been transferred to Slough to take his race-car enthusiasm and mid-engine two-seater knowledge and apply them to Henry Ford II's GT40 project, returned to suburban Detroit to co-found Kar Kraft with entrepreneur Nick Hartman and engineers Bob Negstad and Chuck Mountain. Later, Ed Hull and transmission specialist Pete Wisemann joined the staff.

As engines arrived from Lima, completed car bodies arrived from DAP, and everything came together at a new, larger Kar Kraft facility in Brighton, Michigan, a space leased specifically for assembly of the Boss 429s. Complications arose because DAP refused to build cars without engines even though Kar Kraft didn't want engines. So the Boss 429s came off the assembly line with 428CJ engines installed—the modifications nec-

essary for the CJ package most closely matching what was needed for the big Bosses. These cars were then driven onto transporters, trucked to Brighton, driven off the transporters, had their engines removed, and these were put in storage. To create a Boss 429, some suspension modification was done; the 429 engine was installed; the battery was relocated to the trunk; and the huge, black, front hood scoop was installed along with an engine oil cooler, racing mirrors, and decals. Completed Boss 429s were then shipped back to the Rouge plant for distribution.

Production of the Boss 429s reached 859 in 1969 but declined to 499 in 1970. By comparison, the Boss 302 sold 1,934 in 1969. But the 302 enjoyed magazine reviewer's love of its performance, handling, and balance, and young buyers wanted to identify with the Parnelli Jones/George Follmer racing successes; production jumped to 7,013 in 1970. The Boss 302 was a $676 engine option in 1969, while the 429 added $1,208 to the sticker. In 1970, the Boss 302 became an entire package, selling for $3,720 (compared to the $2,771 base price for a "SportsRoof"—Ford's 1969 and 1970 designation for its Fastback 2+2 body style.) The 429 remained an option and its price went unchanged.

The warehouse of unused, unwanted 428CJ engines continued to fill until, according to An-

The plain 1970 two-door Fastback SportsRoof model sold for $2,771. For an additional $457, one could order the Cobra Jet without ram-air induction, the better to confuse onlookers who wouldn't see a huge hood scoop. For another $205, one received the four-speed manual transmission, and for an additional $155 one was entitled to the Drag Pack option, including the Ford 3.91:1 Traction-Lok rear axle and other internal engine modifications.

Opposite below
It's a quarter mile from the front tires to the farm house. On an average day, the Drag Pack-optioned Cobra Jet 428 with the Ford 3.91:1 rear axle would get there in 14.3 seconds. As it flew past the driveway, it would be running 100 miles per hour. It would reach 60 miles per hour before it was halfway there, in 5.7 seconds.

Always beware of an unadorned car with small hubcaps. It could simply belong to a frugal owner. Or it could belong to someone who has put money into places unseen from the outside. The Fastback SportsRoof lines are perfect to hide the real nature of this Drag Pack-optioned Cobra Jet, or Super Cobra Jet as they came to be known.

thony Young in his book *Ford Hi-Po V-8 Muscle Cars*, the Rouge plant nearly ran out of Cobra Jet engines. Fortunately, Kar Kraft saved the day by shipping back its stored stockpile. A stealth version of the CJ, called the Super Cobra Jet, arrived in 1969, and it was offered only through 1970. However, buyers had to know—and understand—the dealer order forms to find it hidden among option codes. It was not specifically labeled the SCJ but was ordered as the Drag Pack Axle option. The base hardtop or SportsRoof retailed for $2,618 in 1969; adding the Ram Air 428 Cobra Jet was a $420.96 option. After selecting the transmission and whatever other options were desired, adding $155 more provided a few more internal engine modifications as well as a 3.91:1 Traction-Lok rear end. Or, if no-compromise/absolute performance was the goal, spending an additional $52 bought a 4.30:1 Detroit "Locker" differential and rear axle.

Performance options were abundant throughout the last years of the 1960s. If Mustang GT notchbacks with Cobra Jets and Sports-Roofs with Drag Packs didn't satisfy buyers, if Boss 302s didn't have enough grunt, and if insurance costs for the Boss 429 were too much, Ford also offered another jet-flight-inspired option, the Mach I package.

The Mustang Mach I, introduced in 1969, came standard with a 250 horsepower 351C engine with a two-barrel carburetor. Power could be optioned all the way up to the 428CJ with its functional ram-air hood scoop, the 428CJ-R. For the Mach I, the GT390 was only a $100 option; but that was the 390's swan song. It was not offered for the Mustang after 1969. The Mach I came with its own package of appearance cues—hood-pin latches, side body stripes, chromed wheels, and even a chromed, racer-type, quick-open, spring-loaded gas filler cap. The Mach I

with 428CJ-R set the young enthusiast back $3,122 for the car and another $224 for the engine. Prices rose by $149 for the car and $152 for the engine for 1970.

Chassis engineer Bob Negstad, an enthusiast for performance cars, was brought in to replace Matt Donner who had become quite ill, by the time the 1970 Boss 302 was in final development. Negstad had been a part of the Ford Advanced Vehicle crew in Dearborn and was assigned to Ray Geddes to design the 427 Cobra. Roy Lunn and his engineers went to Slough, England, to do the GT40. Once Ford's racing goals

had been achieved, they returned to production car assignments. They discovered that during their absences the committees had made the Mustang bigger and heavier.

Years later, Negstad lamented what happened to the Mustang in the years he and Lunn and others were off accomplishing Henry Ford's competition goals. As he left for England in late 1964, Negstad had heard the clamoring at the doors.

"Everybody in the company said, 'My God! Look at these guys. Look what they've done,'" he recalled, frowning. "And they just came in a rush

1969 Grandé

The Grandé was introduced in 1969 and was offered only as a hardtop body style. It sold for $2,849, and 22,182 were sold in 1969. While wire wheel-covers were standard equipment, the chrome, styled steel wheels were available as an option at $95.31. The car name appeared in chrome script on each side. Many more Grandé models were ordered with the $84.25 vinyl roof option than without it.

While any engine could be ordered for a Grandé, only four buyers checked off the box specifying the ram-air induction, 428-cubic-inch Cobra-Jet engine with its matched close-ratio, four-speed manual transmission. The gearbox was a $253.93 option, and the CJ-R cost the buyer an additional $420.96.

Right
Part of what made the Grandé so grand was its Deluxe Interior Group. This standard equipment package provided extra thick carpets, "Comfortweave" hopsack upholstery with heavy vinyl trim, and wood applique on the dashboard and full-length console. A clock faced the passenger. In addition, the car was virtually silenced with 55 pounds of insulation and sound deadening materials. It was Ford's mini-Thunderbird.

Opposite
The Grandé suspension was known to be on the soft side. In fact, the "Handling Suspension" was not even available on Grandé models and the "competition suspension" was only an option on 428 CJ-R-equipped cars. With something like forty-five options available to Mustang Grandé customers—before they chose exterior or interior color—it's easy to understand how such a rare, personal luxury/muscle car could have been produced.

to take over, and show the troops how it really ought to be done. And every silk-suiter, every politician, every ding-a-ling that was jealous of the success of the people that made the Mustang happen . . . they jumped in and said, 'Wait till we show you how to do this thing!

"And they discovered bigger and larger and heavier and flashier and gaudier. They discovered that as fast as they could discover it." Negstad's frown deepened.

The nice, tight, "together" feel that was achieved with the 1964-1/2 through 1966 Mustangs occurred because of the compromises made in the structure. Structure is a delicate thing: If the structure is too stiff, the car will sound boomey inside; if it's too soft it will shake and rattle and it will not survive a durability test. Adequate stiffness *is* required in order to properly transfer roll stiffness for handling. The structure and tuning of the vehicles is a delicate balance of ride quality and handling quality. Engineers want the twisting characteristics to be a compromise between soft and stiff, balancing the need for stiffness to eliminate shake and to achieve durability against the softness that results in a gentle ride but that may cause body pieces to shake.

Structure is not the only tuning element in the vehicle. Engine mass, engine mounts, and engine damping play a major roll in how the car responds when it hits a bump. The trick is to add the mass of the engine to the unsprung weight of the car to allow the wheels to move without passengers feeling the engine at idle. Softening the engine mounts helps take the engine out of the driver's consciousness as op-

posed to more firmly mounting the engine mass in order to use it in the sprung/unsprung relationship of the suspension.

Minimizing suspension friction is also essential to allow the wheel-tire assembly to move freely over bumps without disrupting the car. Individual components—tires, shocks, wheels, springs, bushings—are the individually tunable items in the complicated equation to balance ride with handling.

"We held on to the '69 and '70 Mustangs, just barely," Negstad said as he brightened some. "The '69 Boss 302 was still one of the finer ones. And the '70 Boss. They were outstanding cars. People that were into cars did those."

And then the frown returned.

"But the baton was passed to a bunch of guys that said, 'Well, if they can do good, wait till they see what we can do.'"

1970 Boss 302
Bob Perkins, in Juneau, Wisconsin, is in the business of restoring Mustangs. He also collects the cars, especially those that have very low mileage and have not been restored. In that way, he can see how Ford Division assembled them originally. This 1970 Boss 302 is such a car, with little more than 1,700 miles on it. In his pursuit of originality, Perkins has also reassembled in his own shop a Ford dealership high-performance showroom.

The Boss 302 sold for $3,720 in 1970, and 7,013 were sold. The car was introduced in 1969 as a Boss engine option, available only on the SportsRoof body style, at $676.15; 1,628 were sold. While most interiors were black, other colors could be ordered. Standard transmission was the wide-ratio, four-speed manual gearbox.

Right
The heart of the package was the engine. It featured strengthened four-bolt main-crankshaft bearing caps, a forged steel crankshaft, and connecting rods and cylinder heads using valves much larger than regular production 302s. Ford fitted a 780 cfm Holley four-barrel carburetor on top of an aluminum high-rise intake manifold. The engine produced 290 horsepower at 5,800 rpm and 290 foot-pounds of torque at 4,300 rpm.

Top left
George Follmer led Parnelli Jones through turn 9 in the April Trans-Am race at Laguna Seca. Following Chevrolet's domination of the series, Ford returned with a vengeance in 1970 with its Boss 302s. *Photo by Bob Tronolone*

Below
The Trans-Am series champion Parnelli Jones swept through turn 7 at Laguna Seca and on through the race series in 1970. Successful racing performances by Jones and Follmer helped sell more than 7,000 street Boss 302s in 1970. *Photo by Bob Tronolone*

Above
The 429 engine was intended—by Knudsen—to establish Ford's supremacy on the stock-car racing ovals. Enough of them had to be manufactured to qualify the engine as a "production" power plant, eligible for use in the Torinos popular on the NASCAR circuit. It is called the "Blue Crescent 429" because its cylinder heads were crescent-shaped, or semi-hemispherical.

Opposite top
1969 Boss 429 and 1970 Boss 429
This could be every Mustang enthusiast's fantasy: two Boss 429s in a barn. At left is a 1969 Wimbledon White model and on the right is the 1970 Grabber Blue version. These cars were a direct result of ex-General Motors executive Bunkie Knudsen's arrival at Ford Motor Company as company president.

Top left
While regular production 1969 Mustangs were introduced in late August 1968, the manufacturing complexities of fitting the wide heavy 429 into the body delayed production of the first Boss 429 until January 15, 1969. To solve the problem, the cars were assembled at Kar Kraft.

Left
Subtle styling differences mark the noses of all the 1969 models, left, and 1970s on the right. Kar Kraft assembled 852 Boss 429s in 1969 and 505 in 1970 through the end of production in December 1970.

Left
Interiors of the 1969 Bosses were standard Mustang fare. Just like with the Boss 302, most of the cars were delivered with a black or white interior, but other colors were available. Buyers could order neither air conditioning nor the automatic transmission.

Above
The Boss 429s were originally sold on Goodyear F60-15 Polyglas tires. While base price for a 1970 Mustang SportsRoof was $2,771, and $3,720 for the Boss 302, the 429-cubic-inch engine added $1,208 to the 302 price. Power steering was a mandatory option as were manual front disc brakes.

Opposite top left
In the Bosses, a black or white interior color choice referred only to seat color and door panels. The carpet, headliner, and dashboard (with the exception of the wood appliqué panels) came in any color the buyer desired, so long as it was black. Between 1969 and 1970, the stitching on the seat changed direction, this being the 1970.

Opposite top right
As wide as this compartment already was, Roy Lunn and his colleagues at Kar Kraft had to increase front track nearly another inch to fit the broad 429. Bore and stroke was 4.36x3.59 inches, and with a 715 cfm Holley four-barrel carburetor and a compression ratio of 10.5:1, the 429 was—in Ford's tradition—under-rated at 375 horsepower at 5,200 rpm while torque was 410 foot-pounds at 3,400 rpm.

Below
The 1969 and 1970 Boss 429s were assembled in Brighton, Michigan, at Kar Kraft. Founded by Roy Lunn and others, Kar Kraft was Ford's "official" race shop. Production reached ten cars a day during the two years the big Bosses were made.

9

"A Thunderbird for the Hell's Angel"
Shelby Mustangs 1969–1970

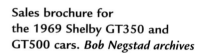

The styling of the 1969 Shelbys faithfully reflected the Mustang family lineage and its breeding. But it was as though a good plastic surgeon—make that fiberglass surgeon—had done more than a few nips and tucks on the body. It required twenty-one separate pieces of plastic and fiberglass to remodel and reshape the body of the Shelby GT350 and GT500 for 1969. One look at the cars made it clear that the emphasis now from Ford was that Shelby's cars should provide good appearance value for money.

Where hood bulges had been a Shelby characteristic in the past, for 1969 the skin was scraped, peeled, sanded, and smoothed. In place of the large, flat, King-of-the-Road nostrils, five National Advisory Committee on Aeronautics (NACA) ducts perforated the hood, gently bending air flow into the engine and evacuating hot air from the engine compartment. Adapted from jet fighters, some of their first uses in automobiles appeared on Ford's GT40 Appendix "J"-car prototype. The influence in Shelby Mustang styling and the actual appearance decisions were coming out of the Ford design center more than ever before. And the GT350/GT500 styling would influence the next-generation production car. Bordinat and his staff were able to try out Shelby appearance cues on auto-show crowds through Ford "dream" cars; the 1970 Mustang Milano bore several elements adopted from Shelby's cars. These would appear directly on—or strongly influence—the final look of the 1971 production Mustang. This included the ducts and the flat, rectangular grille opening.

The standard engine for the 1969 GT350 was the 351W Windsor-built V-8 with 290 horsepower on tap, fed by an AutoLite 550 cfm four-barrel carburetor. (This replaced the no-longer adequate hydraulic-lifter 302 cubic-inch V-8 used only in 1968.) The GT500 carried over the 428 Cobra Jet, still rated at 335 horsepower, still with twin Holley four barrels on top of a medium-rise intake manifold.

Suspension for the cars was essentially a stock Ford Mustang Mach I configuration, with Gabriel Adjust-O-Matic shock absorbers and Goodyear F60-15 Polyglas bias-belted tires. Prices rose again, adjusted by more options being made mandatory to configure the car as a Shelby and as Ford wanted to sell it. The GT350 SportsRoof was base priced at $4,434, with a similarly unadorned GT500 going for $4,700. Of course, dealers—who by and large were offered one single model of each car for an entire year—were inclined to load their Shelbys with options. Fully equipped GT500 convertibles wore a sticker price in excess of $6,300.

The convertibles and SportsRoof models retained the integral padded roll bars, the enclosed cars keeping the two-piece shoulder harnesses introduced with the 1967 and 1968 models. By 1969, the nature of the Shelby Mustang had changed drastically. In 1965 and 1966 the Shelbys were racing homologation specials characterized by *Car & Driver* writer Steve Smith as "a brand new, clapped-out racing car" that Shelby turned out of his Venice shops and his airplane hangars. For 1967 and 1968, the cars were softened and offered in a broad range of exterior colors. By 1969 and 1970 they had metamorphosed into something only vaguely reminiscent of the original race-bred cars. These latter cars offered abundant interior options, were completely carpeted and trimmed with chrome, and wore imitation teakwood on the center console, door panels, and dash.

Sales brochure for the 1969 Shelby GT350 and GT500 cars. *Bob Negstad archives*

Opposite
1970 GT500 Sports Rood
With its long, long nose, it's a striking car. The 1970 price was $4,709, the same as 1969. But with the price of auto insurance rising, muscle cars were beginning to come under scrutiny and their popularity was beginning to fade. Between 1969 and 1970 production, only 1,536 GT500 SportsRoof Fastbacks were sold.

1969 GT350
Exclusivity? The license plate tells it all. One of 194 GT350 convertibles produced in 1969 and 1970. The rear deck lid was fiberglass with a molded-in extension to form the large spoiler. Selling new for a base price of $4,753, it was getting pricey in 1969.

The further the car evolved, the less charitably the enthusiast magazines treated their tarnished hero, Carroll Shelby. *Car & Driver* magazine's Brock Yates wrote eloquently and was a man with enough experience and insider information to understand what Ford Motor Company was up to with the Shelbys. But he also had a strong love of high-performance automobiles and was quite disappointed and upset with the

Shelby's direction. He took out his frustration in print, his text published in contrast to dramatic, eye-catching photos of a new GT350 convertible.

"And so we come to the 1969 edition of the Shelby GT350," Yates wrote, "a garter snake in Cobra skin, affixed with dozens of name plates reading 'Shelby,' 'Shelby-American,' 'Cobra,' and 'GT350' as if to constantly reassure the owner that he is driving the real

The front and rear side air scoops were meant to funnel cooling air to the brakes. On SportsRoof models, the rear scoop sat up higher, near the car's belt line. It had to be lowered on the convertibles to accommodate the roof bows and power-lifting mechanisms.

thing and not a neatly decorated Mustang (which he is)."

Alongside a dramatic photo looking across a vast field of hood interrupted by gentle rises, NACA slots, and NASCAR-style rotating hood lock pins, the caption skewered the car: "The original Shelby GT350 was a fire-breather, it would accelerate, brake, and corner with a nimbleness only a Corvette could match. The GT350, 1969-style, is little more than a tough-looking Mustang Grandé, a Thunderbird for Hell's Angels. Certainly not the car of Carroll Shelby's dreams."

Well yes. And no. The car had gone beyond Shelby's wildest dreams. He did invent "a brand new, clapped-out racing car," a homologation trick in order to go racing and bring glory to Henry Ford II, Lee Iacocca, the Mustang, and the Blue Oval. The legacy that lead to the 1969 and 1970 Shelby styling was huge. But the legacy drew in others, people of power and influence with their own style and taste.

Ford President Bunkie Knudsen was so taken with the 1969 car's appearance that he told Gene Bordinat to integrate the Shelby look into the styling for the 1971 Mustang. Bordinat's stylists in advanced design stretched out new vellum sheets and went to work.

The GT350 used Ford's 351 Windsor with a 470 cfm Autolite four-barrel carburetor mounted on an aluminum intake manifold. With compression of 10.7:1, output was rated at 290 horsepower at 4,800 rpm and torque was 385 foot-pounds at 3,200 rpm. The fiberglass hood held the ducting for the ram-air intake system.

The rim-blow horn was standard equipment. Interiors were black, white, or very rarely, red. Right in front of the driver's eyes were a large 8000rpm tachometer and a speedometer reading to 140 miles per hour. The cars were produced, like the 1968s before them, at A.O. Smith Company in Livonia, Michigan.

The 0 to 60 mile per hour time was 8.0 seconds for the three-speed automatic transmission-equipped car, and the quarter-mile came in 15.59 seconds at 89.09 miles per hour. The convertibles weighed about 3,285 pounds, complete with power-top mechanism and roll bar. The center console was standard as was the AM radio.

Left
For 1969, the hood was a sculptor's delight—or nightmare. Five separate NACA ducts (named after the National Advisory Committee on Aerospace—the predecessor to NASA) perforated the huge fiberglass hood. Only the center feeds the air cleaner and carburetor. The other four let in cooling air and let out engine heat.

On Wednesday, September 3, 1969, Ford introduced its 1970 models, including the carry-over Shelby GT350s and GT500s. For some time, Bordinat's stylists had been frantically pulling working drawings from fronts of 1969 Shelby-based prototypes to use on the 1971 Knudsen Mustang. Then on Thursday, September 11, Henry Ford II fired

Knudsen. It had been a whirlwind 583 days. Some people closer to Henry Ford II claimed it had been too much of a whirlwind. As Knudsen roared down hallways in a hurry to get things done, he stepped on too many toes and bumped into too many egos.

Some of *those* people left Ford. Others threatened to leave or just stepped back, watched the feathers fly,

and waited for the dust to settle. Knudsen's forceful personality and his strong ideas collided with Bordinat and resulted in the next series of Mustangs that resembled Shelbys and Thunderbirds whose noses resembled that of the Pontiac Trans Ams. But what was fatal to Knudsen was that his strengths collided with those of Henry Ford II. And in any given clash of that kind, it is always the man whose name is on the building—and on the paycheck—who wins the fight.

There is another adage in American business. Only fight the battles you know you can win.

One of these individuals who Knudsen bumped into and who threatened to leave was a man of equally strong personality and ideas. He was wiser, however, grown mature by his years of learning from McNamara and working for Henry. Lee Iacocca wanted the job Knudsen had gotten, and he was disappointed when it went outside. However, Iacocca understood better than Knudsen the nature of battles of ideas and egos. Fiercely loyal to Henry Ford II, he rode out the 583 days of Knudsen as executive vice president of North American Automotive Operations. When Knudsen left, Lee Iacocca was still there.

It was to Iacocca that Carroll Shelby turned in the middle of 1969. Shelby, another man of

strong personality and ideas, had also learned the adage. He saw battles closing in around him. The cars that bore his name sold more copies as convertibles with air conditioning than as performance coupes. Even the competition—the Camaro, Trans Am, Barracuda, and Challenger—were selling less muscle and more luxury across the line. Worse yet, he recognized that his own cars were actually competing against Ford Division's Mach I and Boss 302 and 429. Some people within the corporation resented that fact and tried to undermine his influence and his success.

Outside the car-enthusiast world, the voices of public welfare and strident safety activists like Ralph Nader were questioning the need for 300 and 400 horsepower cars. The insurance companies were simply punishing the owners. Finally, the critical comments of friends such as Brock Yates were beginning to penetrate Shelby's tough-as-a-snake skin.

Despite the bitter comments magazine reviewers leveled at the cars, Ford managed to sell 194 of Yates' much-lamented GT350 convertibles, as well as another 335 GT500 convertibles. Sales of the SportsRoof model GT350 and GT500s brought the 1969 total up to 2,364 cars.

With that small figure in mind, everything else on his mind, and knowing that a major new body was due for 1971, Shelby went to Iacocca and Ford Division Vice President and General Manager John Naughton late in the summer of 1969. He asked them to suspend the Shelby Mustang program at the end of the 1970 model year. They agreed.

Throughout 1970, "production" reached only 789 GT350s and GT500s. As Rick Kopec and his thorough researchers reported in the *Shelby American World Registry*, these cars were left-over, unsold 1969 cars. These were given new number plates and fitted with the front spoiler and hood stripes that Shelby introduced that year. This 789 figure was not even a measurable fraction of the record sales numbers that Ford and Iacocca had achieved in the first year of the Mustang. But it was never meant to be.

The Shelbys were always intended to be cars produced for a limited audience with strong, clear, and particular taste. Up through the final evolution, these "personal" cars still fit precisely into the Iacocca Fairlane Committee concept of the Mustang as "Total Performance—Powered By Ford."

Shelby was an exceptional—and very shrewd—innovator. He learned quickly to give the customers what they wanted as well as what they thought they wanted even as he gave them what they needed. He was first to install roll bars and to adopt four-point over-the-shoulder safety harnesses for road-going automobiles in the U.S.

By the 1969 and 1970 models, Shelby's cars were designed and specified as much by the product planners in Dearborn as by Shelby in Los Angeles. More automatic transmissions were sold than manuals. It didn't hurt that Ford had reduced the price to only $30.54 for the optional automatic.

It was the end of the era. This, the fifth iteration of the Shelby Mustang, was the last of the mean muscle. Production of 1970 cars was in large part a renumbering of unsold 1969 models. By the time these cars were being delivered, Shelby had agreed with Ford to discontinue the line altogether.

10

Speeding on Borrowed Time

1971–1973

The pursuit of performance in America—the goal of going faster in an automobile—probably first emerged within a few moments of the birth of the self-propelled vehicle in the United States. Charles E. Duryea and his brother, James Frank, took their first successful drive in their gasoline-powered "motor wagon"—a buggy, really—on Springfield Street in Springfield, Massachusetts, on September 20, 1893. Afterwards, and in the weeks that followed before the first snows flew and inventors' imaginations moved indoors, James Frank had quickly decided that running a one-cylinder, two-cycle, 4 horsepower engine with friction drive just wasn't enough. By early 1894, in the cabin fever of the hard New England winters, he had begun to design a two-cylinder, four-cycle engine to power a new buggy.

Months later in the Midwest, on July 4, 1894, Elmer Apperson ran his first single-cylinder, buggy-bodied automobile in Kokomo, Indiana. With a two-speed transmission, Apperson reached almost 8 miles per hour on the Pumpkinville Pike outside of town. When his buggy wouldn't negotiate the slight incline back up into his shop, Apperson, too, concluded that he needed more power. He began immediately to develop and build an opposed two-cylinder engine to mount on his wagon frame. His goal was to enter—and win—a race sponsored by the *Chicago Times-Herald* newspaper that was scheduled to take place in November 1895.

By April 1895, Duryea's second "motor wagon" had been tested, its new engine backed by a three-speed transmission. Apperson's opposed-twin was running as well. They and the other contestants headed toward Chicago. But on the way from Kokomo for the start, Apperson's two-cylinder was damaged—not the engine but the buggy frame and wheels—, by running over streetcar rails. His original single-cylinder vehicle—also entered—simply was not enough machine to beat the Duryea twin. James Frank won the first official automobile race in the United States, a 50-mile run on Thanksgiving Day, beginning in downtown Chicago and ending up in suburban Evanston nine hours later. Duryea beat a German single-cylinder Benz, the only other vehicle able to complete the distance. And with that endurance race written into the record books, the performance war was begun. It had the same distant effect as a monstrous invasion force massing off the coast but then taking seventy years to hit shore. When it finally hit, though, the battles were ferocious.

However, back in 1895 when that storm first flicked the winds of progress and ambition into the faces of Gottlieb Daimler, Elmer Apperson, and Frank Duryea, the concept of "political correctness" and the considerations of "environmental consciousness" were not imagined. In fact, even in April 1964, uttering those phrases would have provoked in listeners the same blank stares as if they had tried to understand an unknown foreign language. As late as the spring of 1967, when Gene Bordinat's stylists began to dream the dreams of 1971 Mustangs, these two issues did not exist. But as time passed, it would be environmental consciousness that would play a role in the development of the 1971, '72, and '73 Mustangs. And it would be "political correctness" that would redefine the Mustang in the 1980s after the performance war ended.

This poster promoted the legendary 351 Cleveland engine available in all the 1971 through 1973 Mustangs. The poster quoted 300 horsepower at 5,400 rpm. In other literature it has been rated at 330 horsepower as the 351-4V H.O. in the Boss 351 and Mach I packages. In the end it was down-rated to 259 horsepower. *Bob Negstad archives*

Opposite
1971 Boss 351
The 1971 Boss 351 signaled the end of an era. Ford Motor Company officially withdrew from racing on the eve of the 1971 Detroit Auto Show, leaving racers and racing fans alike confused. The car had been conceived as the foundation for a continued Trans-Am effort, and while the 351 Cleveland cost much less to produce than the 302, it became a moot point.

The chassis engineers built a good one, completely revising the front end and steering to accommodate engines much larger than a mere 351C. Front and rear anti-sway bars finished the work done by unequal-length control arms and coil springs up front and the usual semi-elliptic leaf springs holding onto the solid rear axle. This enhanced road feel, and a variable-ratio power steering system improved steering accuracy.

Right
Vacuum-operated ram-air intake vents and ducts cover the underside of the huge hood. This "Dual Ram-Air Induction" was a $65 option to those who avoided the Boss model that sold for $4,124, compared to the plain two-door SportsRoof with its two-barrel 302 at $2,973.

The Mustang that had been introduced to the public for 1967 had grown slightly larger and heavier than its first-generation predecessor. Soon after that introduction, with short- and long-term engine plans already spelled out in countless inter-departmental memos, Bordinat's designers knew only that the car would have to grow larger still. The horsepower war would see 427, 428, and 429 cubic-inch engines force-fed into Iacocca's fourth-generation pony. What's more, product planners and market researchers were returning more and more figures that suggested that, at this time, not only was pavement-rippling, tire-melting acceleration necessary but now it had to come with automatic transmissions, air conditioning, and stereo radios capable of playing a favorite eight-track tape. Oh, and a practical back seat would be nice . . . Say, was real leather possible?

The 428s and 429s had to be *stuffed* into the 1968 to 1970 production cars because no one foresaw that the performance search would culminate in engines so large. Unfortunately, there was not enough time or money to redesign those cars with enough room for service personnel to work on the huge engines. But the engineers and stylists *had* to provide working room for the poor mechanics this time.

The wheelbase for the new cars stretched 1 inch to 109 inches, the first growth in the length of the platform even as the front and rear track spread a second time, another 2 inches up front and 1-1/2 inches at the rear, to 61-1/2 inches and 60 inches, respectively. The body was delivered through more than a dozen full-size clay prototypes until Ford President Bunkie Knudsen saw one on January 18, 1968, and approved it on the spot. By the time it rolled off the assembly line in time for the August 20, 1970, introduction, the body was 2 inches longer and wider than the 1970 model, and it had gained 600 pounds. Much of this came from the weight of optional engines that required extra suspension and chassis pieces.

The styling was striking. Features of the new Mustang teased the buying public; a new Ford show vehicle, the Mustang Milano, circulated North American auto shows beginning in early 1970. This wild purple sparkler adopted the Shelby GT350/GT500 grille treatment that Knudsen had fallen in love with, carried over the Shelby's NACA ducts, and presaged the almost horizontal fastback SportsRoof line.

Engines continued to drive design decisions. The 290 horsepower 302 cubic-inch engine used in the Boss through 1970 was a costly engine to produce; it was replaced with the 351 HO (high output)—the Cleveland—an engine that was a little less complicated, a little less expensive, a little less noisy, and a lot more powerful, developing 330 horsepower at 5,400 rpm. But for pure noise, the 428 Cobra Jet was replaced by a new series of 429s, still called Cobra Jet, Cobra Jet-Ram Air, and Super Cobra Jet (SCJ). The CJ rated 370 horsepower either with the Ram Air induction system or without, while the SCJ was a substantially different engine. With 375 horsepower available at 5,600 rpm, it used four-bolt main bearing caps instead of two-bolt caps (as was common in all the other engines except the Cleveland-built 351 HO), and it relied on mechanical valve lifters (instead of hydraulics used in the other two 429CJs).

The body style formerly known as the notchback was now called the hardtop because the more vertical lines at the back of the roof had been faired out into the deck lid, creating a kind of tunnel behind the rear window. The SportsRoof soon became known as a "flat back" because its line swerved off only 14 degrees below the horizontal. The convertible was carried over and began its eighth season. The Mach I continued in the Mustang line-up as did the luxury model Grandé, both introduced in 1969.

The Boss 351 evolved from the same legitimate racing heritage that had given birth to the 302 and 429 models. It took until opening day of the Detroit auto show, November 21, 1970, to have the new Boss ready for introduction. NASCAR had proposed a new displacement limitation of 366 cubic-inches and the Cleveland-built 351 was to be stretched and developed for that specification. (NASCAR ultimately elected to use intake and exhaust restrictors to limit the power instead of forcing manufacturers to come up with completely new engines.) To keep costs under control for the Boss 351 street version, Boss 302 heads were modified and adapted. The

The 351 had a 4.00x3.50-inch bore and stroke. With 11.0:1 compression and a single huge Autolite four-barrel carburetor, Ford rated the engine at 330 horsepower at 5,400 rpm and 370 foot-pounds of torque at 4,000 rpm. With a final drive ratio of 3.91:1, the Boss was good for 0 to 60 mile per hour times of 5.8 seconds and the quarter-mile took 14.1 seconds at 100.6 miles per hour.

Cleveland engine used a cast crankshaft but forged connecting rods and forged aluminum pistons. An AutoLite 750 cfm carburetor replaced the 780 cfm Holley used on the 1970 Boss 302s. A Hurst shifter operated the four-speed manual transmission, linked to the ground through a locking rear axle.

Ironically, but certainly prophetically, the day before the show opened the *Detroit News* published a story reporting that Ford Motor Company was withdrawing from all auto racing. Anthony Young told the story in his book *Ford Hi-Po V-8 Muscle Cars*. On Wednesday, November 19, Matt McLaughlin, Ford vice president of sales, delivered a formal statement, saying, in part, "For some years Ford Motor Company devoted considerable money, manpower, and energy to the support and sponsorship of various auto-racing activities in North America. We believe these efforts worthwhile as an aid to the promotion of both the sports and our products . . .

The interior gained favorable reviews for comfort, though magazine writers wondered when Ford would provide recliner mechanisms for the front seats. The huge Hurst T-bar shifter fell "readily to hand," as the reviewers described it, and they loved its light, positive feel.

Opposite
Styling of the 1971 models provoked passionate responses. Some observers loved the shapes but criticized the size necessary to accommodate the huge engines Ford President Bunkie Knudsen wanted installed. Others recognized that the car was only an inch longer than the current Camaro and was actually narrower. Critics disliked the nearly flat back window.

"However, we believe racing activities have served their purpose, and [we] propose now to concentrate our promotional efforts on direct merchandising and sale of our products through franchised dealers."

All plans in motion slammed to a tire-shrieking halt. Ford's competition projects that were already in place were pulled off to the side of the track and parked, due to the Thursday, November 20, news story—published, ironically, seventy-five years to the day after James Frank Duryea took America racing for the first time. This was part of the front side of the storm that had already hit Detroit like a one-two punch.

On December 18, the day before McLaughlin's announcement, the Clean Air Bill—a part of President Richard Nixon's National Environmental Policy Act—passed both houses of Congress on a voice vote. This legislation, first proposed during the summer, required automakers to develop an engine within six years that would eliminate 90 percent of exhaust emissions.

In advance of domestic automakers' acceptance of the increasingly strict safety regulations and the emissions standards outlined in the National Environmental Policy Act—to say nothing of the huge costs that implementing these regulations would represent to the manufacturers—

Congress had tossed the car makers and the buying public a bone. The Job Development Act of 1971, passed on November 8, 1970, repealed the 7-percent federal excise tax imposed on passenger cars and made it retroactive to August 15. It was suggested to Henry Ford II and his fellow Americans that this approximately $200 per car reduction would spur auto sales. That was because it would more than offset Nixon's Economic Stabilization Act of 1970 that froze wage and price increases, effective August 15.

When this Act rolled into Phase II, it held maximum wage and price increases to 5.5 percent until April 30, 1974. The battle forces were laying seige to Detroit.

The bombardment hit again in mid-January 1971. This was when the members of the eleven-year-old Organization of Petroleum Exporting Countries (OPEC) reached a deadlock in negotiations with seventeen western oil companies over OPEC's proposed price increases. Together, the eleven member-nations decided to set oil prices themselves, no longer consulting in advance with their customers. Through 1971, the price of a barrel of crude oil would increase in price between 30 and 100 percent. Production and export volume would be cut by as much as 75 percent by the end of 1973. Negotiations would continue, but it would not be before mid-March 1974 that relations between the then thirteen-member OPEC nations and their western customers would calm somewhat. By then, oil that had sold for $2.11 a barrel was going for $14.08. By February 1971, gasoline prices in the U.S. began to jump and skip and by year end, lines formed around gas stations.

Ford money and personnel that had been spent on racing were now needed for more socially, environmentally, and politically acceptable assignments such as vehicle safety and exhaust emissions. Racing had attracted and occupied the minds of Ford's best and brightest engineers and outside talents, beginning with the Fairlane Inn dinners and flowing through Jacque Passino, Roy Lunn, Carroll Shelby, Bob Negstad, and countless others. Those who remained at Ford would be equally challenged by the responsibilities ahead, though nowhere near so satisfied by the achievements.

1971 Mach I 429

The 1971 Mustang Mach I introduced the technology of the resilient urethane front bumper that could be painted in body color. This offered stylists new possibilities in front-end treatments that *involved* the bumper rather than merely treating it as something that had to be added on for safety but would destroy an otherwise successful front-end design.

Below

The interior featured large, prominently placed speedometer and tachometer dials while oil pressure, engine temperature, and ammeter gauges were located in the center pod. Below them, stacked, were ventilation and heat controls, the radio, and a clock. Hurst's shifter and linkage easily accommodated the 429-cubic-inch engine's power and torque.

Opposite

Perhaps the only legitimate criticism of the design of the cars was outward visibility. With high door sills and a low roof line, the driver felt cocooned inside a dark, safe space. The SportsRoof, more a "flat back," dropped only 14 degrees below the horizontal. It was more skylight than backlight. Many current owners recall riding in the back seat as children, staring straight up at trees and stars.

In an effort to postpone what now seemed inevitable, the Boss 351, producing its 330 horsepower in 1971 and using 11.0:1 compression to accomplish that, had to be modified to run on unleaded gasoline for its 1972 production year. Compression decreased to 8.8:1. Power output was reduced to 266 horsepower at 5,400 rpm. Internal changes—significant ones—were necessary to get the engine to run on the lower octane rating, to improve its fuel economy, and to meet all the other emission standards that were already in place. This was what Washington's highest and most influential policy makers had accomplished. This was the effect of what they got Henry Ford II—as the first of the Big Three automakers—to accept.

Sales of Mustangs had steadily declined from its peak of 607,568 in 1966; the numbers slipped to 317,404 in 1968 and down to 170,003 for 1970. The 1971 figures jumped back up to 149,678, this surge partially reflecting renewed interest because of the car's new looks. However, even with the excise tax repeal this upward trend lasted only briefly. Just 125,093 cars sold in 1972. The battle for performance had become a fight for survival.

Throughout 1972, Ford public relations releases and advertising no longer announced horsepower figures or boasted performance statistics. Instead they stated clearly that Ford's engine exhaust emissions equipment cut unburned hydrocarbons by 85 percent and diminished carbon monoxide output by 60 percent.

For 1973, the high-output 351 was a victim of certification difficulties that finally were solved by eliminating most of the small-sales-volume engines. All three 429s had disappeared at the end of 1971, and by 1973, the hottest engine

Top

Much of the appearance of the 1971 Mustangs came from the influences exerted by Ford's new president, Bunkie Knudsen. When Knudsen arrived from General Motors he brought with him Larry Shinoda from GM's design staff. Shinoda quickly began to initiate Knudsen's preferences including the Kamm back end, the flat, cut-off shape developed by Wünibald Kamm in the 1930s.

Below

This is the 429-cubic-inch C-code engine, the non-ram-air induction model that produced 370 horsepower, compared to 375 with ram air. This huge, heavy engine was responsible for the growth of the 1971 car, increasing front track from 58.5 to 61.5 inches because the 429 Cobra-Jet engine with its canted valves was much wider than the 428-cubic-inch CJ it replaced. With this engine and the J-code 429 ram air, weight balance became nearly 60 percent on the front wheels and 40 on the rear.

Opposite

The 1971 through 1973 cars, when isolated from other cars, looked sleek and smaller than they appeared in company. Wheelbase had grown an inch from the 1970 models to 100.9 inches, and length overall had stretched 2 inches, to 189.5. The cars stood 50.1 inches tall and sprawled 74.1 inches wide. With the 429-cubic-inch engine, the Mach I weighed nearly 4,000 pounds.

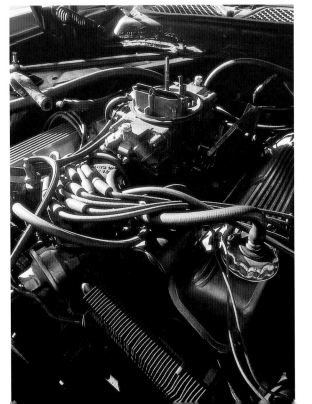

Ford offered was the 351C with a four-barrel carburetor, and 7.9:1 compression that produced 259 horsepower at 5,600 rpm. Emission control equipment—or pollution control, as it was better known—was fitted to all the engines, and in 1973 it included exhaust gas recirculation (EGR) pumps which returned some of the burned exhaust back to the cylinder. This, combined with fresh unburned fuel, reduced combustion chamber temperatures and decreased nitrogen oxides emissions, one of the key elements of smog.

While 135,867 Mustangs sold throughout 1973—up by about 4 percent from 1972—the pendulum that had swung gradually to reach the limit of its range with the 429 Super Cobra Jet in 1971, was now whipped violently back as the last assault hit with full force. At the end of 1973, not only was the 351 deleted from the Mustang catalogs but so was the 302. Back in 1958, the standard 300 horsepower V-8 engine for the new four-seater Thunderbird had been the previous year's largest option when the car was still a two-seater. The last months of the war whipped public reaction completely around Henry Ford II and Lee Iacocca. But the company had prepared wisely, had listened carefully to the warnings, and had studied intently the maps showing the direction from which the attacks would come and looked where they were headed. The aftermath of the dark, brooding skies would reveal drastic change. When the performance war ended, the 1974 Mustang's largest optional power plant would be a V-6 engine. This would displace barely two-thirds of what the smallest engine had for 1973. And it would appear in a car of just about equally reduced proportions.

Opposite

1973 convertible

The convertible was last produced in 1973. It would be a decade—and two chassis changes—before open cars returned to Ford Division's product line-up. Only 11,853 were sold in 1973, but this figure was nearly equal to the total of sales from both 1971 and 1972 (just over 6,000 each year). Publicity surrounding the end of convertible manufacture by U.S. car makers spurred the sales.

Top left

The odometer has not been reset. Owing to sad circumstances, the owner picked up the car but never drove it. Eventually the dealer bought it back and held on to it, knowing that someday, someone would value such a time capsule as this. With every piece of documentation included, every inspection sticker in place, plastic wrapping over seats, and steering wheels intact, it became the ultimate restoration guide.

Lower left

Base price $3,189.00. Total price with all options, $4,066.58. Invoice to dealer, $3,519.14. Delivered to Neilsen Ford in Bloomer in northwest Wisconsin. Financing by the First National Bank. However, as amazing as all this information is to read, the most disheartening discovery is the fact that ten gallons of gas could still be had for $4.

Top

The center console was a $67.95 option. The owner also chose the SelectShift Cruise-O-Matic transmission, the deluxe rim-blow horn three-spoke steering wheel, power steering, the convenience group and the decor group, color-keyed front floor mats, but only an AM radio. The power top was standard equipment.

Lower

The 351-cubic-inch engine used a two-barrel carburetor and was rated at 177 horsepower. It was a $40.79 option. Emissions controls had begun to fill the engine bays that had formerly held 429-cubic-inch muscle engines. Exhaust gas recirculation systems had the most noticeable effect on driveability. However, power front disc brakes were made standard on convertibles.

Opposite

There was no denying that the 1971 through 1973 Mustangs had grown to be big cars. Their lines are as appealing to some as they are off-putting to others. Stockholder Anna Muccioli had challenged Henry Ford years earlier at a shareholders' meeting to bring back the small sporty Mustang. She would soon get her wish.

11

Black Gold and The Little Jewel
1974–1978

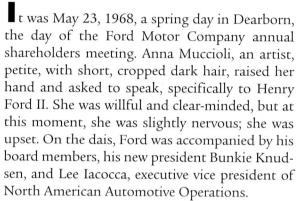

It was May 23, 1968, a spring day in Dearborn, the day of the Ford Motor Company annual shareholders meeting. Anna Muccioli, an artist, petite, with short, cropped dark hair, raised her hand and asked to speak, specifically to Henry Ford II. She was willful and clear-minded, but at this moment, she was slightly nervous; she was upset. On the dais, Ford was accompanied by his board members, his new president Bunkie Knudsen, and Lee Iacocca, executive vice president of North American Automotive Operations.

Anna Muccioli listened patiently to corporate officers outline profits and projects and products, and she waited through dozens of questions from other stockholders about profits and projects and products. And then it was her turn.

"I have just one complaint," she began. "I want to tell you, Thunderbird came out years ago. It was a beautiful sports car. And then you blew it up to a point where it lost its identity."

The crowd, several hundred strong seated in the Henry and Edsel Ford Auditorium, stirred but quieted quickly.

"And now the same thing is happening to the Mustang. I have a '65 Mustang, and I don't like what's happening. They're blowing that one up. Why can't you just leave a sports car small? I mean you keep blowing them up and starting another little one . . .

"You can't see the difference anymore. You don't know Ford from Chevy . . ." She took a quick breath.

"I myself like the look of my Mustang, and I would like to leave it that way. In a few more years I want a new one. I don't want a Chevy look."

Slightly flushed, she sat down in silence.

Henry Ford II was seated at a table with a microphone. He responded to her quickly and warmly.

"I must agree," he began. "From a personal standpoint . . . I think cars could get too big . . .

"On the other hand, what we try to do is to build the kind of car that we will sell most of to the general public, so that is our basic approach to the situation."

Ford kept his eyes on Anna Muccioli. The auditorium was still. "And unfortunately all of the public doesn't like the same thing, and so we have to sort of proliferate here, and hopefully keep in mind what you say here, and have a product that will be satisfactory to you."

She rose again. "Just leave the Mustang small, " she said. "Let's not blow that one up."

The crowd stirred again and then applause rolled through the auditorium. It seemed that quite a few of the other shareholders agreed. Many of them represented much larger holdings than Anna and Joseph Muccioli's 600-something shares.

Ford leaned over to one of his aides and whispered. Muccioli's name and address were in the records. In order to speak, she had had to sign up, to register herself. Anna's husband Joseph worked for Ford, hired in 1951, and by 1968 he was in charge of electrical and climate control in the truck assembly division. Joseph's father had worked for Ford, and their son Ronald was a fairly recent hire as an engineer with Ford.

Was Henry Ford II saying, "if they work here, fire these people," or was he saying, "listen to that applause; this woman has her finger on something"? There is no way ever to know. While the speeches, questions, and responses were

Interior
was Cobra II with its brushed aluminum instrument panel. The King Cobra was offered only with a four-speed transmission. The hatchback was also known as a 2+2, adopting European terminology for the sporty car with occasional rear seats. With the Mustang II, the passengers had to be small or the usage only very occasional.

Opposite
1978 King Cobra
Ford introduced the Cobra II in 1976 as an appearance package that was produced to Ford specifications by Motortown Corporation, an outside vendor in Dearborn, Michigan. By 1977, it was produced in-house. For 1978, Ford took things much more seriously with the King Cobra, supplementing the appearance with better suspension and the 5.0-liter engine to back up the wild paint and graphics.

recorded and transcribed, the quick words from Henry Ford II were not. But Anna Muccioli's words reverberated for the next twelve months, and the echoes didn't die until Ford himself invited Anna Muccioli back in August 1973 so he could show her personally what her comments had wrought.

The small Mustang can almost literally be dated from that meeting. While Anna Muccioli would fret and feel disappointment over what happened to her small sports car when she saw the 1969 models and then even more when she saw the 1971s, she understood Ford Motor Company and the fact that, even by May 23, 1968, the 1971 cars were too far along to change. She knew that production cycles lasted two-to-three years.

It wasn't until GM's former executive vice president, Bunkie Knudsen, left Ford in September 1969 that Anna Muccioli's risk of a Chevy look-alike could be completely removed. Two months later, at a retreat in West Virginia, Lee Iacocca, not yet Ford's president but now its highest officer, reminded his colleagues of Muccioli's concerns, and he expressed his desire that the Mustang change as well. For 1974, Iacocca suggested something sporty, luxurious, and small.

Almost immediately two separate plans were launched under a broader, long-term program known as Project 80. One created a small, sporty car, code-named the Ohio, to be introduced for 1974, built off a reduced-length 1970 Maverick platform. The second would slightly lengthen the 1971 Pinto platform and move it upscale. Called the Arizona, it would be introduced for 1975.

Following the startling success of Ford of Europe's Capri as a Lincoln-Mercury Division import, and influenced by the quick sales and public excitement incited by Datsun's 240-Z, a research team was assembled to take the pulse of small car buyers. Nat Adamson, as advanced product planning manager, organized a show. He and his crew moved a 240-Z, a Toyota Corona, a Chevy Camaro and a Vega, Germany's Porsche 914 and Opel GT, England's Triumph Spitfire GT6 and MGB-GT, Ford's own Pinto, and three full-size fiberglass and metal push around Arizona concept cars into the Long Beach, California, Convention Center. Thousands of market research phone calls resulted in a group of 200 potential customers for this size automobile. They came and looked and kicked tires and slammed doors and concluded that, if Ford built an Arizona, this group would be interested.

Adamson sent his designers and stylists home to their drawing boards to begin the real serious work of fitting interiors and engines into an Arizona. Then he moved his car show south to San Diego where another survey had invited 700 people. These meetings provided similar reactions and results. Unfortunately, through the spring and summer of 1970, Bordinat's stylists were producing cars that were still growing.

Then in November 1970, Ford Motor Company bought 84 percent of Carrozzeria Ghia, the automotive design firm in Turin, Italy. The firm was owned by Argentine art and antique broker and automaker Alejandro de Tomaso, who acquired it in 1966. Ghia and de Tomaso had already created together the Pantera for Henry Ford II. It was to be his Ferrari-killer.

Soon after Ghia was acquired, Ford commissioned it to develop a replacement for the German Capri, and Ghia produced a glassy, classy fastback hatchback. This was a full-size clay model of a car the designers called the Diana, named, it was said, after a secretary who "inspired" many of the designers. It was a visual stretch for American tastes, and Henry Ford II thought it went too far. He scratched into the clay some new lines that he felt better defined Capri, and he left. Iacocca liked the Diana, and after Ford left the studio, he suggested they develop something more acceptable to Ford and to Americans. "I'd like to see," Iacocca said in David Burgess-Wise's 1985 history, *Ghia: Ford's Carrozzeria*, "what you can come up with in the way of a nice little hatchback car in the best European tradition."

Iacocca and Ford returned to Dearborn, and, a month later, Ford and his board of directors elected Iacocca President of Ford Motor Company. Less than a month after that—and only fifty-three days after seeing and rejecting the Diana—Ghia studios delivered a driveable prototype to Iacocca called the Ancona. It stunned Iacocca, both by its looks and by the speed with which the craftsmen had produced something "complete." These effects were lasting.

One question that had been decided soon after the November 1969 retreat was the new-car engine sizes. The V-8 would not be offered. Because this new car would be smaller and lighter, a six-cylinder power plant was ideal. But in-line or vee? Don DeLaRossa, director of advanced design for Bordinat's styling department, disliked the straight engine and argued that it would destroy the compact shape by making the car too long. To make his point, he had an in-line six installed in a modified Pinto frame, and he completed a

The Mustang II was built on a 96.2-inch wheelbase and measured 175 inches overall. The three-door hatchback stood 50.0 inches tall and 70.2 inches wide and weighed just about 3,200 pounds with the 302-cubic-inch V-8 and the T-top roof. While base price was $4,088, with the 2.3-liter in-line four, the King Cobra was closer to $6,800!

The front air dam, hood scoop, rear deck-lid spoiler, the black grille, and the King Cobra logos and graphics were all part of the $1,277 option. Many—but not all—of the King Cobras were built in Bright Red, but the full Mustang II color line-up was available. The graphics decals and tape stripes made Dearborn Assembly Plant personnel crazy.

mocked-up Arizona, done well enough to drive and finished well enough to paint. Bill Innes, promoted to replace Iacocca as North American Automotive Operations executive vice president, loved the car. That was the bad news. The good news was that he recommended that the Ohio project, which was proceeding parallel to this Arizona car, be ended. In July 1971, Arizona became *the* 1974 Mustang. Well, not exactly. There were still the thousand usual details. Except in this case the details were huge. DeLaRossa hadn't finished fighting the engine battle. That meant the shape and styling of the car were still undecided.

DeLaRossa created another full-size clay model representing how the car would look with an in-line six under its hood. Immediately after Iacocca had commented internally how important it was to make the next-generation Mustang small, DeLaRossa invited him over for a look.

The strategy worked. Iacocca killed the straight six, and out of this was hatched an all-new 2.3-liter four-cylinder engine and a slightly enlarged version of the Capri's optional V-6. The

in-line four would be assembled in the Lima plant, known previously for 429 Bosses, and would be Ford's first four-cylinder engine since Henry Ford II's father authorized the last Model B in 1934. It would also be the first metric engine built in the U.S. Though more or less derived from Ford of Europe's 2.0-liter Cortina engine, this new one was so completely redone that only nuts and bolts could be shared. An overhead camshaft fit within its iron head. A two-barrel Weber-Holley carburetor fed fuel through an aluminum intake manifold. Horsepower was rated at 102 at 5,200 rpm with compression of 8.4:1. Total engine weight was quoted at 319 pounds. The optional V-6 was a bored-and-stroked version of the 2.5-liter Capri engine, enlarged to 2.8 liters. This engine made 119 horsepower at 5,200 rpm with 8.2:1 compression.

Once DeLaRossa cleared the engine hurdle, the decision on the car's appearance still had to be made. Again, with unsatisfactory responses coming from Styling, Iacocca proposed another contest, this time inviting the newly acquired

Ghia studios to participate as well. Fifty clay models were carved and shaped, developed out of 150 drawings proposed before the end of the three-month deadline. In December 1971, the final candidate from the Lincoln-Mercury design studio was a fastback with a tapered waistline below the door window. Design chief Al Mueller's staff had created a car that bore many Mustang cues, including a front-end treatment and side scoops strongly reminiscent of the 1964-1/2 model. Iacocca loved it, finally choosing it over his own favorite, a notchback coupe done by Don DeLaRossa based on Ghia's notchback Ancona.

With this obstacle removed, the matter of body styles emerged most clearly. Ghia had provided both a fastback and a notchback coupe. Should Ford continue a convertible? Should they offer only one coupe style so as not to confuse buyers with too many choices or distract them from the message that this is a different car? Customer sampling was inconclusive. Surveys in Anaheim, California, virtually killed the notchback. Southern California's love for sportiness strongly favored a fastback Arizona. But a last-minute decision to include the ill-favored Ancona notchback (nicknamed the Anaheim in honor of its failure there) in a last-minute San Francisco survey turned the tables completely. This was three months *after* Iacocca had decided the car's appearance. It demonstrated the difference between audiences. The Anaheim-reject scored most highly up north. With work already begun on the fastback by that point, DeLaRossa's notchback was back in. Plenty of work was needed to redesign the notchback to make big sheet-metal items such as its hood and doors common to both cars. It was now only sixteen months before Job One.

Another obstacle. What to name the car? Arizona was its code. But it was important that car buyers understood what this car meant, that they recognized that Ford Motor Company was alert and responsive to trends and to their desires. Other names were never seriously considered. Lee Iacocca once told *Motor Trend* writer Karl Ludvigsen that his most important "personal" contribution to the Mustang II was "the name—not changing it."

Iacocca husbanded this new car as patiently and attentively as he had the first car a decade earlier. He understood "perceived value," and he wanted this new car perceived as "a little jewel." Some four-cylinder cars from other makers suffered from buzzy engines and from uncomfortable, harsh rides. Iacocca wanted customers to perceive of his little jewel as a diamond, not pressed glass. Glass rode like small cheap cars; diamonds rode like limousines.

Four-cylinder engine vibration would be unacceptable in the jewel. At certain engine speeds, a harmonic vibration set up a moan that ran through the car. Enlarging the diameter of the bolt circle to mount the engine to the transmission changed the harmonics and reduced the noise and vibration. This was a change made late in the development, a modification that cost millions. Using a stronger, 3.5-inch diameter drive shaft rather than the Pinto's 2.75-inch diameter shaft, was the final polish to the gem. The slight additional mass of the shaft further dampened vibration.

To come up with the primary specifications for the Arizona, engineers had cut a 94.2-inch wheelbase Pinto in two pieces right behind the windshield and lengthen it 2.0 inches. Real luxury-car ride and handling would have required starting from scratch, something for which there was neither time nor budget. Making the Pinto

The 5.0-liter (302-cubic-inch) V-8 was shoehorned into the Mustang II beginning with the 1975 model year. With a two-barrel Autolite carburetor and 8.4:1 compression, *Hot Rod* magazine recorded 134 horsepower at 3,600 rpm and 247 foot-pounds of torque at 1,800. Final drive was 2.64:1, yet this was enough to cover the quarter-mile in 16.59 seconds at 82.41 miles per hour.

The 134 horsepower could be delivered with enough enthusiasm to spin the Goodyear 195/70R13 radials. Performance from 0 to 60 miles per hour took about 11.2 seconds. Front power disc brakes and rear drums stopped the King Cobra, and stabilizer bars front and rear helped keep it flatter while cornering.

ride, handle, and drive as an Arizona jewel fell to program engineers Jim Kennedy and Bob Negstad.

"If you take a Pinto," Negstad recalled, "and you just change the name and the emblem, it's still rides just like a Pinto. We kept showing the car and riding the car. Everybody that rode it said, 'Hmmm. It feels like a Pinto. And we want it to feel like a little jewel.' One of 'em even looked at me once and said, 'And after all, we gave you a Pinto to work with. What else do you need?'"

Negstad grimaced, shrugged, and waited two beats.

"And so we struggled and strained. We were not getting anywhere. I was working for Charlie Vranian, an old-time Ford engineer. Been around for a long time. We're trying this and that, and we're trying, you know, double isolated tension struts and double isolated number-two cross members. And we're changing geometry. And we got, ohhh, I'm up to trial number fifteen or so. And we're building cars. And we're riding them. And they're terrible cars. They're just bad cars. They're just not a good car.

"And finally, Charlie came down one day and he said, 'I'm gonna throw in the towel. We don't have a viable solution to doing the Pinto. We'll make the . . . we're gonna vote to make the Mustang carry over.'"

This meant going before Vranian's boss, Stu Frey, chief engineer for all car lines, who would go before his boss, who would go before his, and finally someone would have to go before Mr. Iacocca and recommend to him that Ford Motor Company *not* introduce a new Mustang, not introduce a new little jewel for 1974 because it still rode like a Pinto.

"All the politicians were all gathered around," Negstad remembered. "They all had their oars in the water, ready to stir things up, to paddle away, so I told Charlie, 'I've got one more idea. It probably won't work, but as long as we're all gonna go down . . .

"'I want to take *all* the reactions of *all* these input loads—the potholes and bumps and curbs and corners—and spread them over the floor pan, not the front rails. We've got to get the loads out of the front rails. They're too highly loaded, too stiff. We've got to get it back to the floor pan.

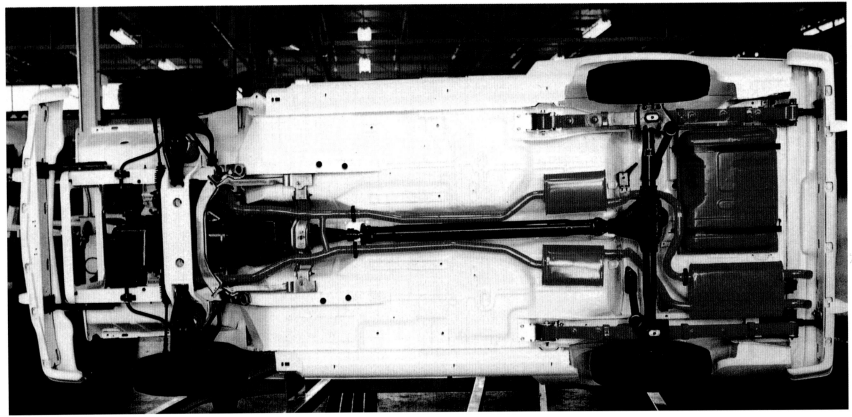

Once the "toilet seat" was completed and approved, Bob Negstad had it painted yellow-gold so it would stand out more dramatically. This was the substructure that gave Lee Iococca's little jewel the mini-limousine ride the Ford boss wanted. *Photo by Bob Negstad*

"Oh," he said, "I know. But how're you gonna do that?"

"I dunno, Charlie, but cut me some slack."

This was on a Friday. Vranian authorized overtime to bring in a crew on Saturday and Sunday. After Monday, it would be too late. And everybody went home and returned early Saturday morning.

"We started. We're cobbling this thing up out of anything, any piece of scrap we could find in the welding room. We're designing with a piece of chalk on pieces of scrap iron. The welder's cutting it out with a torch. We got guys drilling holes. And they're all shaking their heads saying, 'Well, at least, we're gonna get to the end of this, we're gonna get to go home at last.

"We designed a little device that was rubber-isolated all the way back to where the rails kicked up [about at the firewall]. Used compression biscuits—like hockey pucks—that reacted into that thing. When the wheels reacted, it let this whole thing move around and average all the loads before it came into the body. It looked like hell," Negstad chuckled.

"We got it together. Put the car down. It was Sunday. Late. I went for a ride. And my god, it didn't feel like a Pinto. I sent the guys home, told 'em I was optimistic. They couldn't believe this piece of scrap junk. Then I called Charlie at home. He came in. It was very late Sunday.

"We rode it. We went home.

"We came back in Monday morning, early. Rode it again. We brought some more people over to ride the car. And at noon, it went across the street for a management review.

"We were basket cases. We said, 'We have a proposal that we think meets all the needs and helps the image of the car. We're not proud of it but . . .

"At the end of the meeting, the Company said, 'It's a good idea, it's affordable. We still gotta crash it, gotta do some other things.' And then we had a design review. There were no drawings, there was only . . .

"We took this thing off the car. It was all dirty. There was a can of yellow spray paint, and I spray-painted it yellow lacquer. And we grabbed it and took it over and took a piece of paper and put it on the table. Chassis Engineering said, 'This is the piece? That's gonna save the Mustang?

"And it got the nickname. Cause of its shape. The 'toilet seat.' And that lasted a long time, and it looked just awful and it went into production."

What it did was allow all the front wheel shocks to be absorbed by this "toilet seat," which also carried the engine. This sub-assembly actually used the mass of cast iron as part of the damper. Then this piece was attached through a number of the hockey pucks to the traditional car frame.

All the while Negstad worked on the front end, Jim Kennedy toiled at the back. He eventually revised the "iso-clamps" by changing their material, compression, and by increasing their size. He replaced the rear-spring tip liners with a material far slipperier than anything else available. He enlarged the front spring bushing diameter and isolated the bracket from the frame. He enlarged the bushing on the top of the rear spring shackle. This went further to isolate any spring input to the rear of the chassis that might come from potholes or uneven surfaces. In addition, he replaced the rear universal joint pinion mounting flange (using a full-circle flange that allowed eight mounting positions instead of the normal four).

Kennedy selected front engine mounts—big and soft—to isolate the engine vibration at idle that would otherwise be felt through the pedals and steering column by the driver. He specified highly damped "Herclor" power-steering rack-mounting bushings. Finally, he used a new isolator for the steering coupling connection between the input shaft for the rack and pinion and the steering shaft. This product was developed by an outside vendor that also made women's foundation undergarments.

Dick Allen, Larry Halstad, and the other engineers, all specialists in the art of sound packaging, pursued a limousine-like silence inside car. They ultimately installed more sound deadening and insulation material into the Ghia package than was used in a Lincoln Continental. The search for isolation and insulation to create a little jewel knew almost no bounds.

By the time Allen, Kennedy, Negstad, and the rest of Charlie Vranian's and Paul Nyquist's engineers finished, all that really remained of the Pinto was its rear wheel houses, the trunk floor, front suspension arms, and the rear axle. It was less of a Pinto than the '64-1/2 had been a Falcon.

For Lee Iacocca, this was the re-invention of his dream. Ford staff designer Charles Keresztes created new Mustang logo sculptures that ran in the same direction as before, but these horses were somewhat smaller. Viewer samples and marketing surveys once again pointed toward this being the right car at the right time. It was, to quote Casey Stengel, "déjà-vu all over again."

Ford began leaking information and even pictures of the new car, officially named Mustang II by Ford's public relations staff in an internal memo, in August 1972. Iacocca publicly hinted that this car was of such high quality and that it was so exciting that it might exceed the phenomenal first-year sales record of the '64-1/2 Mustang. Henry Ford II himself invited Anna Muccioli—and of course, the local press—for her own private preview of the car. She saw a white notchback with its white vinyl roof, a model called the Ghia that replaced the luxury Grandé. A foot shorter than Muccioli's 1965 Mustang and not even 300 pounds heavier, including luxury equipment and new pollution and safety features, the new car impressed her. "Now that's more like it," she beamed. "That's the kind of car it started out to be." She posed for pictures and allowed that she would sell her '65 and replace it with a Mustang II.

By the time it hit show rooms in September 1973, the public had once again been let in on the secret. But this time, they were underwhelmed. This was not quite the scale of betrayal as the Edsel, but buyers, anxious to see Iacocca's little jewel, found dealerships showing models of the $2,895 notchback that were fully optioned and wearing price stickers in excess of $4,500. A stripped car at anything less than $3,000 was nowhere to be found. Buyers muttered, shrugged and while some settled for the hatchback Pintos or two-door Mavericks, others left.

Barely 18,000 cars sold in the first month, very disappointing compared to 22,000 on the first day in April 1964. The enthusiast magazines were none too enthusiastic about the mini-limousine Ghia or the four-cylinder Mach I. Weight distribution was equal to the 1973s—58 percent

The 1978 Mustang II "Monroe Handler" was a project car that originated in late 1977 with *Hot Rod* magazine. Eight identical cars were built by Dave Kent and his southern California firm, Creative Car Craft. The wild bodywork for the prototype was not fiberglass but metal and required some 300 hours of form making, hand pounding, and machine rolling to achieve the shapes. Molds were made to reproduce the seven additional show cars.

front/42 percent rear—and 2.8-liter track tests yielded 0 to 60 mile-per-hour times of 13.8 seconds and quarter-miles of 19.4 seconds at 70.5 miles per hour. Even the optional engine didn't get the car moving out of showrooms. Through mid-October slightly more than another 17,000 cars had been ordered.

Three days after mid-October, the Mustang II began to look very appealing all across the United States. Morning newspapers reported that OPEC, in protest of U.S. foreign policy related to Israel, shut down the pumps and turned off the spigots on oil deliveries to the West. The gas lines that briefly appeared in 1971 came back in

frightening proportion as gasoline and heating-oil producers predicted gloom and doom. The White House responded with talk of gasless weekends, no driving on Sundays (something Germany did put into effect for a short while), and a national "energy-saving" speed limit that slowed traffic from 70 and 75 miles per hour to 55 miles per hour for years to come.

Five months later, on March 18, the Organization of Arab Petroleum Exporting Countries (OAPEC) ended the embargo. President Nixon's price controls had allowed two small increases that still fit within the 5.5 percent cap each year, so by year end, the $2,895 notchback was up to

$3,134. The Mach I fastback with optional V-6 was listed at $540 more. Despite the slow start, the year's sales total was not bad, aided immensely by the increasing cost of gasoline. By September 1975, sales totaled 296,041, more than twice the 1973 big Mustang level.

The most exciting improvement for the car's image was the arrival in 1975 of the 302 cubic-inch V-8 engine (available for any Mustang II but with automatic transmission only). The new Mach I, ordered with the Rallye suspension package, offered adjustable Gabriel shock absorbers, and it included larger-diameter anti-sway bars and stiffer springs. Handling was much improved as a result, and the extra power cut 0 to 60 mile per hour times to 10.5 seconds and got the car through the quarter mile in 17.9 seconds at 77 miles per hour—still not neck-snapping. However, Washington was beginning to notice fuel economy. Corporate Average Fuel Economy (CAFE) performance standards were another concept that was talked about. Each automaker would be required to meet fuel economy quotas across their entire fleet, that number increasing each year.

For 1975, the Mustang II offered an MPG model, with a 3.18:1 rear-axle ratio (compared to the standard 3.40:1) and fitted with a catalytic converter—required on all cars destined for California delivery. Highway mileage was quoted as 34 miles per gallon whereas city performance was 23 miles per gallon following the EPA standards for testing. This kind of fuel efficiency counterbalanced the more profligate consumption of the 302.

For 1976, the catalytic converters went nationwide. Fuel economy for all Mustangs was improved. The 302 now was available with a four-speed manual shift, this combination having completed its mandatory 50,000 and 100,000 mile EPA runs. In addition, a Cobra II appearance option was offered, but it was savaged in the magazines, mostly because it was offered with the four-cylinder engine as standard equipment. However, careful reading of the options list—just as in the late 1960s—could turn the little Cobra into a reasonably exciting mini-muscle pony.

Beginning in 1976, the public began to accept gas prices around $1 per gallon. It was not that salaries had risen by 200 to 300 percent as gas prices had done, it was simply that the United States is a nation of drivers. In America more than anywhere else—largely because of the affordability of gasoline—driving is recreation. Going for a drive is a pastime. Relationships begin, matrimony is proposed, families start, and marriages end inside automobiles. With the acceptance of higher gas prices and the continuing drama of interpersonal relationships inside a moving "neutral territory," the desire for larger, roomier cars resurfaced. Mustang II sales slipped again, to 178,541.

For 1978, performance was coming back. Flamboyance was reintroduced with a promotional Mustang II sponsored by the Monroe Auto Equipment Company. This car—actually a steel-bodied prototype and seven identical fiberglass copies—was produced to promote Monroe's new performance product, the Handler shock absorber. The cars eventually became showcases for the works of well-known and not-so-well-known fabricators, painters, and suspension and chassis men—with ample help from Monroe—and an am-

The one steel-bodied prototype and the seven fiberglass "production" Monroe Handlers started life as 1977 regular production Mustang Cobra IIs. By the time Dave Kent's bodywork was finished, Trevor Harris's suspension was done and Jack Roush's engine was built, the creative juices had been spent. The Cobra II interior remained largely untouched except for the addition of the Monroe Handler badge.

Next page
Inspiration for the bodywork was pure-IMSA race car. Paint was pure show car. Primed first with white epoxy, it was guide-coated with black acrylic lacquer, then wet-sanded away. Acrylic lacquer was used for the body color, and this was wet-sanded and then air-buffed, and a plexiglass polish was applied to complete the finish.

ple 363W from Jack Roush Industries, quoted at 400 horsepower at 6,500 rpm. Writer Gray Baskerville longed for the car in the third of *Hot Rod* magazine's August/September/October step-by-step production stories. "Ahh," he cooed, "it's like shades of yesteryear."

Yesteryear was coming back strong. Ford Division knew it and was prepared as 1977 ended with even smaller sales numbers. Only 161,654 Mustang IIs moved out of dealer showrooms until September when the 1978s appeared.

During the previous years, the Cobra II had turned into a respectable small performer. Enthusiast interest in the Monroe Handler was rewarded when the King Cobra was unveiled. It was a $1,277 option that, among other ingredients, provided buyers with a very high recognition factor among local police. It looked outrageous. It even performed pretty close to outrageous, with a 302 cubic-inch V-8 and Variable Venturi Carburetor, an effective combination for fuel economy consciousness and performance potential. The purchase price included a huge Pontiac Trans Am-style decal laid out across the hood, the removable-panel option SportsRoof, a rear anti-sway bar, stiffer springs, and adjustable shock absorbers. Horsepower was rated at only 139, but that was under new SAE standards that measured "net" horsepower, that is, power actually transmitted through all the running gear to reach the ground. It was a much more accurate measure of engine output, but it drastically deflated egos when King Cobra owners had to answer the question they dreaded most: "How many horses you got under the hood?"

The Environmental Protection Agency (EPA) finally introduced its CAFE (Corporate Average Fuel Economy) specifications for car makers (these affected a manufacturer's entire fleet), which began at 18 miles per gallon for 1978. It was to be 20 miles per gallon by 1980, and by 1985, Uncle Sam wanted the entire production run—average of all cars by all makers—to be 27.5 miles per gallon. Total 1978 Mustang production rose again, reaching 192,410. A very high proportion of the 2.3-liter four-cylinder and 2.8-liter V-6 cars counterbalanced the mileage numbers developed by the roughly 5,000 King Cobras that were produced and sold in the last year of Iacocca's little jewel.

The buying public knew that a new Mustang was coming for 1979. The country had endured a kind of performance dark ages through the mid-1970s. In the period between September 1969 and September 1979, everything in America got turned around. Gasoline prices jumped a full dollar, from roughly $.20 per gallon to one $1.20. Engines got huge and then cars got small. Engines got small and then cars began to grow. Skirts rose and fell. A President who was re-elected later resigned, and his successor would later be voted out of office as the country's leadership changed political parties and tried to change course. In early 1974, Daylight Savings Time was adopted year round in an attempt to save heating

fuel and gasoline, but it was soon repealed. Ironically, in an era of growing fossil-fuel consciousness, clothing and textile manufacturers promoted a new fabric that was highly wrinkle resistant and somewhat stretchy. It was called polyester, and it was based on petroleum products. In 1975, after twenty years of trying to protect South Vietnam from North Vietnam, U.S. forces evacuated. And a year after that, in 1976, North and South Vietnam reunited as one country in a hideous mockery of the hundreds of thousands of lives lost keeping them separate. Soon after that, supersonic flights shrunk the world for well-heeled travelers between Washington and London or Paris, cutting ten-hour flights to five hours. But

The black trim was not chromed nor anodized. It was a semi-gloss black paint that was baked onto the trim at 500 degrees. Maremont Corporation's Cherry Bomb mufflers and BFGoodrich GR50-14 T/A radials on Centerline 8-inch front and 9-inch rear wheels and hours of handpainted sponsor names finished the car.

Racing engineer Trevor Harris, builder of numerous Can-Am and Trans-Am winners, tackled the task of making the Monroe Handler handle. The front end was lowered 2.5 inches, using custom coil springs, and the rear 1.5 inches, using shorter leaf spring shackles. The front anti-sway bar grew 0.125 inches in diameter, to 1.125 inches. And, of course, Monroe Handler shocks were fitted all around.

the sleek, startling Concorde was allowed to go no further West because of its noise. The energy shortage took on a new meaning when New York City blacked out in late summer 1977. Some parts were dark or without refrigeration or air conditioning for as much as twenty-five hours. The U.S. Department of Energy was established in 1977, and in the late spring of 1978, a new baby boom erupted in New York City, a result of excess energy of another kind that came with the heat and the dark. A few months later, in the middle of the summer of 1978, a supertanker, the Amoco Cadiz, ran aground in a North Atlantic storm and spilled 220,000 tons of crude oil that washed ashore to darken and damage 110 miles of France's sea coast.

Just as Ford poised to introduce its new Mustang, cult leader Jim Jones led nearly 1,000 followers in Guyana to drink poison Kool aid and within a month, the exiled Ayatollah Khomeini called on his millions of followers to overthrow the Shah of Iran.

It was through these times that Ford engineers and stylists, product planners and marketing surveyors, Lee Iacocca, and Henry Ford II gazed once again into a crystal ball. They had begun looking for this new direction as early as 1972, just as Volkswagen replaced its long-lived Beetle with its Golf, known in America as the Rabbit. Throughout Dearborn, what Ford people imagined running after the rabbit was the Fox.

A Mustang II like no other—or like only seven others. This is a Jack Roush-prepared 302 "improved" to 363 cubic-inches. While suspension and chassis modifications were slight, engine modifications were monstrous, including a 351 Cleveland crank that added 30 cubic-inches in one move. Output was rated at 400 horsepower-plus at 6,500 rpm, with 400 foot-pounds torque at 4,800 rpm.

12

The Worldly Fox
1978–1984-1/2

A Ford Mustang Just Beat A Porsche. Why Is That So Surprising?

Advertising "comp" dummy produced by Wells, Rich, Greene, Inc., to promote additional racing victories by Ford's SVO Mustangs. *Bob Negstad archives*

Opposite
1984 Twentieth Anniversary Edition Turbo GT 350 convertible
One of the rarest of Fox-chassis Mustangs is the 2.3-liter turbocharged convertible. Only 104 were produced out of an entire production of 5,260 GT350 commemoratives. (Barely 350 turbo coupes were built while 5.0-liter convertibles numbered 1,213 and 5.0-liter coupes were almost abundant, with 3,333 produced.)

No product is conceived in a vacuum. The development of any idea is subject to countless unavoidable outside influences.

Ford Motor Company had produced cars in Dagenham, England; Cologne, Germany; and in Poissy, France, a suburb of Paris. Each factory produced a different automobile, unique to some extent due to the character of the country in which it was manufactured. But another view suggested that some Ford car ideas remained in foreign markets because they seemed ill-suited to the U.S.

Now the world was shrinking, and Hal Sperlich had an idea.

An analysis had been made. Ernest R. Breech, the man who for years was Henry Ford II's mentor and his company's president, initiated it and then codified it. Born in the Missouri Ozark mountains, Breech learned accounting at night school, and his first job was in 1925 working for a Chicago businessman who had decided to expand his Yellow Cab service into a car rental. The businessman promoted his new idea by using a distinctive color combination. When John Hertz's black-and-gold taxi and self-drive car manufacture was acquired by GM a year later, the twenty-nine-year-old Breech went with the deal.

Breech was among the first to understand the accounting principles of cost analysis, and, ultimately, this led him to become GM's problem solver. GM-supplier Bendix Corporation was losing $3 million a year in 1937 when Breech was sent there. Within two years of his arrival, it was earning $5 million a year in profit. Henry Ford II knew that his father's company was in financial trouble. Losses of as much as $50 million were acknowledged, but accounting discipline was so lax that there was no way of knowing where the losses originated. Ford coaxed Breech to join him as executive vice president in July 1946, several months after Robert McNamara and the Whiz Kids were hired. Breech, forty-eight by then, had the skills to save Ford's company, and Henry II, at twenty-eight, was sharp enough to learn from his new teacher.

Cost analysis taught Breech that the size of a corporation was a function of the investment in production facilities. This meant that however large the existing facilities were, they allowed the manufacture of x-number of cars; a company could not build twice that number without doubling the investment. By the same token, the company could only sell as many cars as it had dealers. It was possible to sell as many cars with slightly fewer dealers but to sell twice the number of cars, the company probably needed twice the number of dealers.

Breech's analysis, which seems almost simplistic forty years later, went further. It would encompass insight and prediction.

Ford Motor Company had attempted to take on General Motors, "to be first in America," as Breech once explained, by adding the Edsel to its structure as a complete, separate division. Ford's failure with the E-car set the sizes of Ford, General Motors, and Chrysler into relative proportion: All of Ford Motor Company would sell about as many cars as Chevrolet Motor Division of GM would sell; all of Chrysler Corporation would sell about as many cars as Ford Division sells. And probably Nash-Hudson and Packard-Studebaker would sell as many cars as Plymouth Division would sell. For Ford to sell more cars, it would be necessary to move into a new marketplace, in this case Europe. This was more effective than fighting with General Motors and fighting off

1979 Indy Pace Car replica
The new Fox chassis featured body styling supervised by Jack Telnack. Early proposals showed a fastback extending all the way to the end of the body. But Telnack's sense of proportion, finely honed in Europe as head of styling for Ford in Germany, moved the angled line forward to create better aerodynamics as well as a more distinctive look.

Right
Mustang's second pace-car appearance at Indianapolis came for the 63rd running in 1979. The car was as different from the previous Mustang II as the first production car in 1964 was from Ford's other products. Something like 11,000 replicas were manufactured.

Chrysler; Ford should simply expand into the world. McNamara's Cardinal was Ford's first attempt to make a "world" car.

The styling of the Cardinal, so far as Lee Iacocca was concerned, killed it for U.S. sales. The success of the Mustang distracted Henry Ford II from the world market for a short while. It returned his focus to the pursuit of Chevrolet. But even the phenomenal sales of Iacocca's pony car had not been enough to overtake Ford's competitor. Ford came to believe that he could beat General Motors only if he hired General Motors—in

the person of Bunkie Knudsen. Knudsen's magic, that shine of a GM-insider that would rub off simply by his being around, didn't provide the sparkle Henry Ford II was looking for. In the end, Knudsen had come to rub Ford the wrong way. The idea of bringing GM into Ford in order to beat GM had failed. With no more faith in quick fixes, Ford knew the next attempt would require plain old hard work. As it rolled up its sleeves, Ford Motor Company began once again to look seriously at Europe.

Hal Sperlich, the product planner whose ideas *had* made a difference, got involved near the end of 1972 in a committee that looked at a world driven by petroleum. The committee understood that the availability of petroleum was now subject to the political whimsy of a group of exporting countries that could be easily offended. The group inside Ford considered what would happen if it all got worse.

In April 1973, the Environmental Protection Agency (EPA) released its first set of recommended gas-mileage ratings for automobiles. Buyers, however, gained a better appreciation for the numbers in October 1973 when the Arab oil embargo was begun. Ford's timing with the introduction of its more gas-conscious Mustang II was perfect. But that car would take Ford only so far, through 1977 or 1978.

Meanwhile, Hal Sperlich—like Ernest Breech before him—had in his mind a car for both Europe and the United States. The same car would sell on both continents. Same engines, same suspensions, same bodies. It would be fuel-efficient, and it would also be manufacturing- and cost-effective because parts would be interchangeable throughout the world. Casting molds and stamping dies would be the same. This project, to develop a common platform that would support both a sporty car as well as a four- or five-passenger sedan, was launched early in 1973. It was code-named the "Fox" program.

Ford of England had planned to replace its Cortina, and Ford of Germany was looking for its next Taunus. Also at this time, Dearborn was conceiving new cars to replace the Pinto, Mustang II, and Maverick. The Fox was the platform of choice for the U.S. (while the Escort/Sierra were chosen for Europe). Design and development began in the summer of 1973 on a shorter wheelbase—100 inches—to respond first to the need for the Pinto/Cortina/Taunus. Through the next year, work advanced the Fox/Pinto platform, and it was begun on a Fox/Fairmont sedan. But by then—1974—problems in achieving Sperlich's theoretical world car became readily identifiable. Safety standards differed from country to country, and no nation was willing to yield it's regulations to another's. Hugely different production techniques between European and U.S. factories in the size of their body panels, in spot-welding philosophy, as well as in proprietary characteristics of their outside vendors' components represented the final insurmountable hurdle to the same-car-everywhere project at that time. But the platform on which to base a Pinto/Mustang/sedan was looking more and more viable. By spring 1975, North American Automotive Operations (NAAO) had taken over the Fox program from Sperlich's Product Planning and Research.

The first Fox Fairmont prototype was a reworked yellow English Cortina. It was transferred to NAAO with a torsion-bar MacPherson front

The 140 horsepower 5.0-liter V-8 first appeared in the 1975 Mustang II. Power remained unchanged, although numerous changes improved cold start, driveability, and fuel economy. What was new was the four-speed-plus-overdrive manual transmission offering a 0.70:1 gear ratio in fifth. Carburetion was still only a two-barrel.

suspension and a side-arm four-link rear suspension designed by Bill Allison (a former Packard chassis engineer/suspension inventor working at that time for Hal Sperlich).

"It was an idea that was great with a frame," Bob Negstad explained. "But it's not a good idea with a unitized car. The loads are too concentrated."

These loads would require quite a bit of additional structure, or reinforcement, all the way to the middle of the car. That translated to extra weight which would defeat one of the purposes of unitized construction in the first place. With a unit body, the torsion bars would have to be perfectly made, exactly balanced. Ideally, they should be adjusted *on* the car *after* it has taken its set. It was tricky, heavy, and expensive, none of which fit the cost or weight targets.

"MacPhersons generally have the spring surrounding the strut. We couldn't do that," Negstad continued. "There was no room for that. When you do that, you have a high fender and structure to support it. And the image of the car was to have a low cowl, hood, and fender height. So we came up with this hybrid MacPherson.

"I worked with a guy named Bob Burns. We got to noodling one day. 'Why don't we just take the torsion bar off, throw it away?' I wondered. 'And put on a cheap steel coil spring?'

"We got to looking at the Chevy Nova front suspensions. They had a nice, neat, clean front-suspension lower [control arm], and a compact, efficient coil spring. It was cheap and simple and light and packaged and all that.

"Burns went off and bought some Nova springs and front-suspension pieces from the Chevy dealer up on Michigan Avenue. From petty cash. Came back, and we scrounged in the experimental garage for some other pieces that looked about right. Made some drawings. And went into the computer and figured out some spring and suspension points."

Negstad and Burns took their Chevrolet Nova lower arm and, then they modified it to fit a Ford ball joint. The cross member was redone to attach to the Ford unibody. Retaining Chevrolet bushings, it was welded into place.

"And without a lot of fuss, we took off the torsion bars and put on the spring, reacting in the cross member. And it was right the first time we put it on the ground."

The rear suspension adopted the four-link design that was well-proven. A rear anti-sway bar stiffened up the back end to make the car handle neutrally rather than strongly nose-heavy in a turn or an emergency maneuver. This became standard equipment on the Fairmont and all 1979 Mustangs, the bar's diameter varying from smallest with the standard equipment in-line four cylinder up to the 30mm bar on the V-8-equipped Fairmont police car.

As an authorized, approved, and funded program, NAAO set introduction dates: the new Fairmont sedan for 1978, and a new Mustang for 1979. (It deleted the Pinto from the Fox program altogether, although its cost and weight objectives were carried over. The most noticeable effect of this was a lack of funds to improve the dashboard and other interior features in the Mustang.)

As the specifications for the new Fairmont/Mustang were being set, Gene Bordinat's designers and stylists started to work. While this might be a U.S.-only automobile, NAAO wanted European influence to be recognizable, both in determining the car's appearance and its handling. The Fox would respect "world" car concerns such as fuel economy and overall size and weight even if the "world" car was not practical at that time.

"Hard points"—the basic measurements that could not be altered—were decided for wheelbase, tread width, overall length, height, width, cowl, radiator heights, and other dimensions. These specifications virtually defined the shape of the car. Ford, Lincoln-Mercury, Advanced Vehicle Development, and Ghia design studios all began to create the appearance of the Fairmont sedan and the Mustang. Early proposals for the Mustang from Fritz Mayhew, Light Car Design manager, were striking. These wedge-shaped sports cars with large glass areas appeared to be derived more from de Tomaso's Pantera than from any existing Ford product. After the hard points were established, however, the appearance was less daring. Each of the proposals bore some resemblance to the others, and most all of them had hard, tall, flat sides because of sharing the basic structure of the Fairmont sedan.

Jack Telnack returned to Dearborn in April 1976. He had spent the previous several years in Germany as design vice president for Ford of Europe. Telnack—promoted to the position of executive director of North American Light Car and Truck Design—and his ideas arrived like a breath of irreverent fresh air. Telnack simply cheated.

Hard points were considered inviolate. So—after careful consideration—he moved two of them. To Telnack and his counterpart in engineering, Bob Alexander (promoted to product development vice president), the "real" hard point of the new car's front end dimensions was the height above the ground of the engine's air cleaner. Anything else might not be so hard.

Telnack wanted to lower the nose, to decrease the car's frontal area in order to improve its aerodynamics, and to increase its fuel economy. Lowering the nose was possible by pivoting the hood line over the air cleaner. This meant raising the back of the hood, at the windshield. It startled management because, as Telnack told author Gary Witzenburg, "No Detroit designer ever asks to make anything higher." But Gene Bordinat agreed to try it, knowing it would require a different support to lower the radiator (and understanding that it might eventually cost more than $1 million to develop). At the same time, Engine Engineering was pressured to lower the intake manifold as well as the air cleaner to help the hood line.

Telnack went ahead and slightly narrowed the nose as well. Fender wells were swelled somewhat at the axles, furthering the interest of aerodynamics and giving the car a very slight Coke-bottle effect. Telnack also favored a louvered grille treatment that induced better airflow through the radiator. But customer clinics disliked its appearance.

Styling again relied on clinics to test the potential customers' reactions. Consistent with a dozen years of Mustang, the audience was nearly equally divided on their preference for coupes or fastbacks. Following these late winter and spring sessions, Telnack's crew came up with the idea for a "semi-fastback," a design slightly more reminiscent of the 1965 and 1966 cars than the 1967-and-later SportsRoof full fastback design.

In fact, while a number of early proposals for the Fox Mustang had carried over the design cues of the early cars—especially the side scoop that had become almost a trademark—there was only one really striking similarity: Just as had occurred with Dave Ash's designs for the '64-1/2 cars, the 1979 car arrived in the dealer show rooms virtually unchanged from the Telnack proposal.

He had proposed that the fastback deck wrap around the body, similar to what had been done on Honda's Accord and VW's Scirocco. Manufacturing balked because they had never done one that way before, and they were concerned about maintaining the exposed fit line on the rear deck and body side. But Bob Alexander insisted and the idea was approved.

The Telnack styling of the 1979 Mustang proved its design merit. When it hit the University of Maryland wind tunnel that Ford was using for its testing, the rear deck resulted in a 6 percent reduction in drag.

By September 1976, the first three engineering prototypes were available for development. Besides ride and handling, a major concern for Glen Lyall and his engineers—Joe Cezair, Jim Aldrich, Jim Murray, and others—was the noise, vibration, and harshness (NVH). These had been thoroughly addressed in preparing Iacocca's little jewel, but the Fox was a completely different platform. The prototypes were put through the same "durability" tests that had broken the 1964-1/2 cars and had necessitated the "toilet seat" on the 1974 Mustang II. But the Fox Mustang had the advantage of the Fairmont development lead time and of the work done to develop its police car and taxicab versions.

Where Ford Mustangs had been exclusively shod on U.S.-made tires in the past, the shrinking

This poster announced the return of the 5.0 liter engine with the arrival of the 1982 model year. *Bob Negstad archives*

The front suspension used a modified MacPherson strut, system that relocated the coil spring off the strut and a front anti-sway bar. Three suspension systems were offered. The Indy Pace Car replicas and the Cobras were equipped with the top-of-the-line Special Suspension incorporating Michelin's TRX low-profile tires and metric cast-aluminum wheels. Shock absorber valving, front and rear springs, and front and rear stabilizer bars were exclusive to the package.

world and the European experiences of Telnack and Alexander suggested to chassis engineers that other tire options deserved consideration. Michelin's high-performance TRX and a metric-dimension wheel had been tested for some time within Ford Motor Company. Mustang engineers concluded the work with three separate chassis options: a handling package that would introduce the TRX tires, an intermediate version that would use a variety of domestic and imported mid-level radials, and the baseline car that would be delivered with bias-ply tires.

Sedate performance was tolerated in Iacocca's mini-limousine, vinyl-roofed Mustang II Ghia, introduced in 1974. However, the pursuit of performance was once more an admirable goal. Six engines were available, from the baseline, 2.3-liter, overhead cam, in-line four cylinder carried over from the Mustang II, up to the now-ten-year-old 302 cubic-inch (5.0 liter) V-8. High technology from Europe brought a turbocharger to the 2.3-liter four. It produced a lightweight engine package with 132 horsepower that provided much better weight balance than the more-powerful 302.

The turbo was a mixed blessing. On the one hand it provided the high-end horsepower that a V-8 might, but without the heavy fuel consumption. On the other hand, at lower engine speeds, such as getting off the start-line when the turbo was not up to operating speed, the engine simply moved on its own four-cylinder torque. This latter disadvantage is the result of how turbochargers function. Once the turbines spin up to speed—80,000 to 100,000 rpm—the fuel/air mix is literally force fed into the combustion chambers and the engine produces power quickly, even suddenly. However, it takes the building of exhaust gas pressure to turn the turbines and the more exhaust gas, the more spin, hence the infamous turbo "lag." At the time, only a few car makers—Porsche, Saab, and Buick—offered turbochargers, and they were only beginning to understand the relationship between the length of exhaust pipe the gas traveled through to get to the turbo and turbo lag. In a nutshell, the longer the pipe, the greater the lag. Magazine tests of the turbocharged Mustang recorded 9.1 seconds for 0 to 60 miles per hour and quarter-miles in 17.4 seconds at 82 miles per hour. (In comparison, the 302's best performance was 8.3 seconds to 60 miles per hour and 17.0 seconds at 84.8 miles per hour.)

Coupled with oil lubrication problems that caused some turbos to fail and others to ignite, it was a great idea whose time had not quite arrived. There was much to learn, and it would be several years before the 2.3 Turbo would become a performance package to reckon with.

The enthusiast magazines were invited to Dearborn for the annual ride-and-drive introductions of the 1979 cars in mid-June. Writers liked the new styling and the car's size (overall, it was 4.1 inches longer, and its wheelbase was 4.2 inches longer, yet it weighed nearly 200 pounds less than the comparable 1978 model). Magazines interested in handling and road-holding praised the Michelin TRX package but criticized the weight bias (60 percent front/40 percent rear) that the car suffered with the 302 cubic-inch V-8. Those publications that only promoted short-distance, straight-line travel loved the 302 but felt the Michelins were not up to the torque that the engine produced. The rear tires broke loose and hopped until the car caught up. As with the turbocharger, getting all that power to the ground would take some work and require some more time.

A month later, as journalists toiled with their stories and editors tried to match product release dates with print schedules, all of them—daily newspapers, television news, and magazine editors and writers—were sent back to their newsrooms. Stop the presses, tear out the front page. On July 13, 1978, Lee Iacocca was fired from Ford Motor Company by Henry Ford II. He was allowed to stay three months, until his fifty-fourth birthday, to enable him to qualify for full pension benefits. The ebullient salesman, the brilliant strategist, the steadfast supporter of the Mustang, was—most of all—a profound loyalist to Henry II. However, the charismatic Iacocca had become more identified with Ford Motor Company than the aristocratic Ford himself. Ford had learned everything he could from Ernest Breech, having in the end promoted and elected him to chairman of his board. At Ford Motor Company annual meetings, Breech spoke

for Ford's company. In July 1960, having learned enough to speak for himself, Ford accepted a resignation from Breech that many people understood he had elicited. As Iacocca recalled in his 1984 autobiography, Ford prefaced Breech's firing by saying, "There comes a time when I have to do things my way."

Henry Ford II's 1979 Mustang had been out a full month by the time Lee Iacocca's grace period expired. The car Iacocca had nurtured and supported like his own child was in its teens. It already had a kind of maturity. It had always worn Henry Ford II's name, and Ford had learned his lessons well from Ernest Breech. There would be no last-minute tinkering with success.

The third-generation car was offered as a two-door and three-door (meaning fastback/hatchback) coupe. The upgraded trim and appearance option was still named after Ghia studios. List price for the two-door with the baseline 88 horsepower, 2.3-liter, four-cylinder engine was now up to $4,494. The 2.8-liter German V-6 was carried over from the Mustang II and was available for $273, and a new 200-cubic-inch (3.3-liter), 85 horsepower, in-line six was introduced for $241. The 132 horsepower turbocharged engine was a $542 option while the 140 horsepower 302 was $514. A "Cobra" package included the turbo-four, TRX

The steering wheel wore the early Ford Motor Company logo while the instrument panel resurrected the machine-turned appearance of racing cars from the 1930s through the late 1950s. This was also used in the new 1979 Mustang Cobra. The full instrumentation was part of the GT package. Special checked-cloth upholstery was used on the Recaro bucket seats in front and the fold-down rear seat. The Recaro seats were completely adjustable.

tires and wheels, and two paragraphs of additional description including badges and spoilers and paint, for $1,173. One other option replaced an entire body style. The "flip-up, open-air roof," was a hinged sun-roof for $199, and it was as close as 1979 buyers could get to a full convertible.

Fifteen years after the first Mustang appeared at the Indy 500, the new Fox was chosen to pace the race on Memorial Day 1979. Goodyear ties with the Speedway forced Ford to adopt Goodyear Wingfoot tires, but the chassis needed only slight modification for the change. In order for the pace-car driver and assistant to be seen by the racers, the car and its identical backup got prototype T-roofs, as well as fully adjustable Recaro seats and a number of spoilers, wings, and graphic treatments. Ford hired racer/engine magician Jack Roush to produce pace-car 302s, capable of running—in a worst-case scenario— much longer than a full 500 miles at 125 miles per hour. The two Roush 302s used forged steel crankshafts and connecting rods left over from Boss 302 parts bins, and better breathing four-barrel carburetors were mounted atop aluminum high-rise manifolds. Roush fitted larger intake and exhaust valves into 351 Windsor heads to replace the stock 302's. Automatic transmissions were revalved and rebuilt to handle the speed and power—Roush's 302s developed more than 260 horsepower compared to the street cars' 140—and larger front disc brake rotors and oversize rear drums replaced the stock issue.

To commemorate the occasion, Ford Division produced another 11,000 Indy Pace Car replicas, lacking, however, the Roush running gear modifications. They did keep the form-fitting Recaro seats, thereby introducing reclining buckets to the Mustang. In all versions, Ford sold 369,936 Mustangs through the 1979 model year (nearly twice the 1978 total of 192,410).

For 1980, the Cobra option included the Recaro seats as well. This—as the good news—*almost* compensated for the bad news under the hood. In efforts to close in on Ford's CAFE figures, the big pony was forced to run with one broken leg. The 302 was reduced in displacement to 255 cubic-inches by decreasing bore from 4.00 to 3.68 inches. Horsepower was downrated from 140 to only 119. Ford continued

The Indianapolis 500 Pace Car replicas were offered only as three-door hatchback models. However, they could be purchased with the lift-up sunroof or the removable-panel T-top. The graphics were applied either by the dealership or by the owner after purchase.

1984 Twentieth Anniversary Edition Turbo GT350 convertible

Carroll Shelby was nonplused when Ford resurrected his GT350 designation to commemorate its twentieth year in production. While Shelby had sold Ford rights to use the Cobra name, the deal did not include the GT350 or GT500 titles, and Ford agreed to quit after this one limited run.

through 1981 with the 2.3-liter Turbo (which by this time was its most powerful option, still at 132 horsepower), but problems with reliability forced it to be withdrawn at model year end. Base prices rose slightly, to $4,884 for the two-door coupe with an 88 horsepower four-cylinder, and ranged up to $5,512 for the Ghia three-door. The 2.8-liter V-6 was dropped, leaving only the 3.3-liter in-line, up-rated to 91 horsepower. The 255 cubic-inch (4.2 liter) was a $338 option.

The Cobra package still included the 2.3 Turbo (for $1,482), but if buyers chose instead the 4.2 liter, they were credited $144. Mid-year, Ford introduced a much-welcomed four-speed-plus-overdrive (effectively five speeds) manual-shift transmission. On the auto show tour, Ford showed its Mustang IMSA, named in honor of the International Motor Sports Association, the sanctioning body in which Ford Mustangs were being qualified for competition. Under the hood, Ford installed the 2.3 Turbo. It looked very stock except for widely flared wheel wells that barely contained enormous Pirelli tires. It served as an announcement. While advertising beginning in 1979 promoted the new line of cars as "The Next Generation," there were a great number of racers and enthusiasts glad to see hints of "Total Performance" again. In all, through 1980, total sales were 271,322.

The May 1979 Indy official pace car T-roof was offered as a $916 option for 1981. While early brochures listed the 2.3 Turbo among engine choices, Ford Division withdrew it just before the 1981 introduction. Only three engines were available: the base 2.3-liter four-cylinder with normal carburetion; the 3.3-liter 94 horsepower six-cylinder; and the 4.2-liter V-8 which, with its two-barrel carburetor, rated an embarrassing 120 horsepower. The five-speed transmission introduced during the previous spring could now be mated to a Traction-Lok rear axle, a limited-slip differential without the noise and aggression of the late-1960s versions, that finally addressed the wheel spin and brought axle hop under control. The Cobra package, now available with only the 4.2 liter, was discontinued at the end of 1981. The two-door base sedan was listed for $5,897 while the three-door Ghia was published at $6,901. The Cobra option was down to $1,071, the Traction-Lok cost $71, and the Recaro seats sold for $776. Altogether, Ford sold 182,552 Mustangs for 1981.

Some time in 1981, aftermarket car stylists and body shops began cutting the tops off T-roof coupes and cobbling together not-always-good-looking convertibles. Individual operators and even small corporations that lacked the budget to prepare full-size clay models produced cars with incorrect proportions. The best of the shops understood the chassis-stiffening requirements of an open car. Modifications cost as little as $1,000 and as much as $5,000. Ford Division noticed but did not respond publicly to this trend or these privateers.

Completing 50,000- and 100,000- mile engine-emission certification runs kept test drivers and engineers busy. Various engine, transmission, and rear-end possibilities were registered and certified with the EPA. But the effort paid big

dividends to enthusiasts when the catalogs were published for the 1982 Mustangs. Ford re-introduced the 302, now called the 5.0 liter H.O. (high output) and rated at 157 horsepower. In addition, it brought back the GT package—available in either red, black, or metallic silver body paint with spoilers and a large hood scoop (albeit cosmetic, not functional).

Body designations changed as two-door coupes got more substantial "B" pillars and became two-door "sedans." Ghia's name disappeared, and in addition to the GT, there were the L, GL, and GLX packages. Pricing ranged from $6,345 for the two-door L sedan with base 88 horsepower, 2.3-liter four, up to $8,397 for the GT including its 5.0 liter H.O. with a five-speed transmission. The TRX tire, wheel, and suspension package was $111 for the GT, and adding Recaro seats cost another $834. The T-roof was $1,021. It was the first year that a fully-optioned Mustang would crack the $12,000 barrier.

If 1982 had been good for power and performance, 1983 was good for the spirit. Ford Division re-introduced the convertible after a ten-year hiatus. No longer would the T-roof have to serve to air the cobwebs out of overworked brains. A flip of a switch below the dashboard lifted the top back out of the way or returned it to the windshield. The all-glass rear window folded itself. Overnight, legions of body-shop men with cutting torches were put out of the convertible conversion business.

The engine line-up was broadened. The 3.3-liter in-line six was dropped, replaced with a new 3.8-liter V-6 rated at 112 horsepower. Performance engines also were more plentiful. The turbo returned, now as part of the three-door Turbo GT package. With 145 horsepower on tap, it had been quite thoroughly reworked, benefiting from the adoption of Ford's new electronic fuel injection. But more appealing to American street racers was the 5.0 liter H.O., which replaced the insufficient two-barrel carburetor with an updated 1980s version of the 1960s Holley 600 cfm four-barrel. Horsepower was rated at 175.

To keep this power on the ground, GT-package tire size ballooned from the 185/75R14 radials out to 205/70 high-speed-rated radials. The base two-door L sedan was listed for $6,727 while

No intercooler aided this metric-specification, 2.3-liter, single overhead-camshaft four-cylinder engine. With bore and stroke of 3.781x3.126 inches (96.0x79.4 millimeters), 8.0:1 compression, and a two-barrel carburetor, it produced 145 horsepower at 4,600 rpm, with torque of 180 foot-pounds at 3,600 rpm.

Below
The Twentieth Anniversary model was offered only in Oxford White with red interior and trim, such as the rocker panel tape designation. Tires were Michelin TRX P220/55R390s, and the cast-aluminum metric wheel package, introduced with the Fox chassis in 1979, was offered through 1984. The package was worth a $27 credit on the GT350 in lieu of the Goodyear Eagles that would replace them from 1985 on.

Top
Promotional one-sheet given away to race fans to promote interest in the Mustang GT Enduro entry in IMSA. *Bob Negstad archives*

Top
Promotional one-sheet given away to race fans to promote interest in the Mustang GT Enduro entry in IMSA. *Bob Negstad archives*

Below
In the high desert 150 miles northeast of Los Angeles, every surface is either protected from the hot direct sun or it is damaged by it. Covers on the dash and seats here mask damage already begun. Full instrumentation, a "sport" steering wheel, and manually operated articulated front seats were all part of the GT option included in the Twentieth Anniversary package.

MUSTANG GT ENDURO

the GT convertible represented a significant splurge: $13,479. But at that price, very few options remained except for air conditioning, and few buyers in the early 1980s were so decadent as to need air conditioning *and* open air. The price for the three-door Turbo GT was announced at $9,714. The appearance of all the cars changed slightly due to a redesigned grille and taillights. Sales totaled 120,873 cars.

For 1984, Ford introduced its Twentieth Anniversary GT. This bore the logo GT350 just where it had been nineteen years earlier. It was offered with either the turbocharged in-line four, still developing 145 horsepower, or the 5.0 liter H.O. Available as a three-door sedan (at $9,774 for the 5.0 liter, $9,958 for the 2.3-liter version) and a convertible (for $13,247 and $13,441), the cars were strictly Oxford White with Canyon Red stripes and interior. A total of 5,260 were built as open and closed cars.

For noncommemorative cars, both the 3.8-liter V-6 engine and the 5.0 liter H.O. replaced their environmentally temperamental carburetors with a new throttle-body electronic fuel injection. While it decreased the horsepower rating of the 5.0 liter from 175 to 165 horsepower, it improved everything else from cold starting to

throttle response to fuel economy. In addition, a sophisticated onboard engine management system was introduced for all 1984 Fords. Called the EEC-IV (Electronic Engine Control-fourth version), it furthered Ford's pursuit of ecologically conscientious performance.

On April 17, 1984, some 500 Ford Mustangs congregated for an enormous show and new product introduction. In the center of the Griffith Park Equestrian Center polo grounds near Burbank, California, Ford Public Affairs staff carefully directed owners and collectors to their parking spaces, forming a design they could only see later that night on local and national television news. A circle surrounded a giant number twenty, the shapes made of Mustangs. News media helicopters buzzed overhead.

Celebrities in the best of the Hollywood film and entertainment tradition turned out and told stories of first dates and first kisses and first loves in Ford Mustangs.

Commemorative GT350s, new electronics, and old tales told out of school weren't the only developments revealed in mid-April 1984. A small group of dedicated people had been at work since 1980, taking the Mustang in a very different direction. Their car was created outside the mainstream. Hal Sperlich, who had left Ford in mid-1976, was not there to see the "world" car influences that came home to Dearborn. The new car struck some enthusiasts as the same kind of breath-of-fresh-air as when Ford re-introduced the convertible. Others never understood it and didn't want it.

The two-door turbo GT convertible sold for $13,341, nearly $3,500 more than the turbo GT coupe. By 1984, Ford had taken convertible production back in-house at the Dearborn Assembly Plant. The turbo was not too popular because the 5.0 liter High Output (H.O.) developed 30 horsepower more yet sold for about $200 less.

13

Deviating from the Straight Line

SVO Mustangs 1984–1/2-1986

Ford's Back.

Show the layout, it is not to be read. Sample copy is not to be read the purpose is to show this type face and size in the layout. Not to be read. Sample copy is not meant to be read the purpose is to show this type face. Sample copy is not to be read. It is read, the purpose is to show this the layout. It is not meant to

It's Miller time

There's A Ford In America's Future.

The Mustang IMSA show car was the tip of a small iceberg floating a short distance away from Ford World Headquarters on the south side of Dearborn. While the show car was meant to announce the return of Ford to racing, it became much more than that to groups as vast and diverse as Mazda Motor Company and the United Auto Workers. The IMSA show car meant that Ford was going racing with its pony car. This meant that Ford was going to continue to build it.

There had been some discussion in late 1980 that Ford Division would allow the Fox platform to run out its usable life as a Mustang and then Mazda's Probe would be imported and it—four-cylinder engine, front-wheel drive, and all—would be the 1983 or 1984 Mustang. The plan advanced far enough that plants supplying parts for the Mustang were reassigned to manufacture for other vehicles. The axle plant was to turn out axles for Ranger trucks, for example, while Dearborn Assembly Plant would begin assembling other automobiles. While it seemed to make financial sense, it struck some people within the company as profoundly wrong.

The question it raised was the one that has defined the Mustang ever since 1962 when Roy Lunn advanced the idea of a lithe, sleek two-seat GT curve-hugger for the youth market. This was America where the kids on the corner got their future girlfriends' attention by squealing their tires. Lunn lost his fight and the Mustang became a smoke-the-tires, Main Street racer. The die was cast, its image set.

For 1980 there was nothing else in Ford Motor Company's line-up that squealed its tires while Chevrolet Division alone had two, its Camaro and the Corvette. Ford concluded that it could not afford to change the Mustang so radically by nothing more than badge engineering. So, soon after

one series of directives reallocated factory space and employee hours, another set was issued, rescinding the first ones. The Fox Mustang would be carried over at least through 1985. Quickly the date was moved back through the 1987 model year. And so the iceberg that had been launched in 1980 with a single, modest show car, was set free to sink or swim.

There was a skipper for this craft, a German who had run Ford of Europe's racing program as director of Motorsports through the 1970s. He had commanded memorable performances from small cars called Zakspeed Capris. When Ford Division concluded that it was time to take Ford Mustangs racing again in the United States, Michael Kranefuss was invited to come to Dearborn and command the effort.

Ford had learned some painful lessons after that cold November 20, 1970, day when it abruptly withdrew from all racing participation. Its credibility in that world was shot. Now, in 1980, it heard from privateers who told horror stories of trying to race Ford engines during the past ten years, but having difficulties in getting parts. Others recounted experiences of individual Ford racers ten years earlier who competed not only against Chevrolet and Chrysler or against Ferrari and Porsche but also sometimes against Ford Motor Company. And of course, after November 1970, when Jacque Passino was ordered to have all the racing spare parts scrapped. . . Privateers had come to disbelieve in Ford factory racing support.

So Kranefuss was given the difficult task of trying to re-establish Ford's reputation. He was named director of a small group of dedicated engineers, designers, financial people, and marketing and public information personnel, who would perform this miracle under

Advertising "comp" dummy produced by the Wells, Rich, Greene, Inc., agency to announce racing victories scored by Ford's SVO Mustangs. *Bob Negstad archives*

Opposite
1985 SVO coupe
The SVO was designed to accommodate flush "aero" headlamps. Following its introduction in mid-1984 with standard sealed beam headlights, it was not until late-June 1985 that models were able to take advantage of a relaxation in federal standards that allowed aerodynamic "composite" headlights—meaning those with a separate bulb and lens/reflector system. The 1985 SVO sold for $14,806.

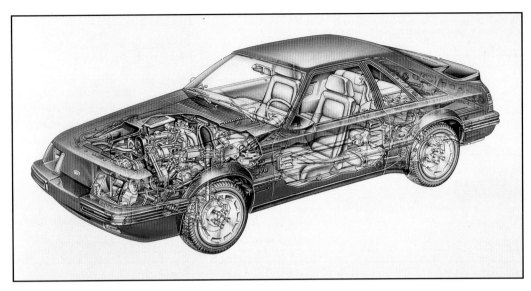

Cutaway drawing of the 1984-1/2 SVO Mustang. *Bob Negstad archives. Reproduced by permission, Ford Motor Company*

Right
The addition of the air-to-air intercooler (in between the Garrett AiResearch turbocharger and the cylinder head) produced a 30 horsepower gain to 174 horsepower at 4,500 rpm, with 210 foot-pounds torque at 3,000 rpm from the 2.3-liter electronic fuel-injected in-line four-cylinder engine. Power remained the same for 1985, but in mid-1985, dual exhaust, a wilder camshaft, and increased turbo boost lifted the power to 205 horsepower at 5,000 rpm and 248 foot-pounds at 3,000 rpm.

the name of Special Vehicle Operations, SVO. (Ford Division had paid attention to the ways and the speed with which outside "vendors" such as Ghia design studios, Jack Roush's organization, Kar Kraft, and Dearborn Steel Tubing got things accomplished. Even though SVO was part of Ford Division, upper management thought that putting it outside the Dearborn "campus" might enable it to operate more efficiently.)

Part of SVO's considerable support came from Walter Hayes, formerly manager of Public Affairs for Ford of Europe. Hayes, a distinguished Englishman, had controlled—under the umbrella of Public Affairs—the purse strings for the GT40 program. While the racing in Europe benefited engineering developments, it was furthering Ford's image. Following Ford's successful—and repeated—attacks on Le Mans and on Ferrari, Hayes was transferred to the U.S. and named Vice President–Public Affairs.

The analogy of an iceberg is partially accurate but perhaps partially unfair. That only the surface was visible, that the great mass that supported it was revealed only to those who knew where to look is a fair characterization. It was not kept secret but it was not widely publicized that SVO was supported by Hayes' Public Affairs' budgets. Furthermore, a successful racing program at home might distract public attention from the Pinto following a tragic rear-end accident in which the gas tank ignited. Where the iceberg analogy suffers is in the fact that icebergs move without direction, piloted by the wind and ocean

currents. This cool, efficient floating mass with its European skipper had a rudder and it had a course to follow.

Kranefuss was given three goals for his task. First, SVO was to encourage Ford involvement in Motorsports and to supervise its activities. This was to be done through a small factory effort with Mustangs. It was also to select promising private teams and provide them with a great deal of assistance, in parts, technical backup, and even in financial support. Second, SVO was to expand the racing- and high-performance street-parts program, marketed under the banner of Ford Motorsports.

The third part of SVO's "mission" was to develop and produce a limited-issue, high-performance passenger car that would translate SVO's racing success to the streets of America. This production car would also generate the profit necessary to fund the racing programs without requiring further assistance from the corporation.

By mid-1982, SVO and Ford Motorsports had spread octopus-like tentacles into every form of racing in the U.S., from NASCAR to showroom stock to Indianapolis to the prototype category of IMSA. It had also decided what its "production" car would be.

Glen Lyall had been brought in to SVO as Engineering Manager, and Bob Negstad was imported as chassis engineer because he had, by that time, twenty years experience making Mustangs handle. That was to be his job on SVO's car that was invented to handle well more than anything else.

SVO's racing efforts were carried out with a turbocharged and intercooled version of Ford's 2.3-liter overhead camshaft, in-line four-cylinder engine. A detuned version of the racing engine was to be developed for the street car. It would introduce multiport fuel injection to Ford engines and intercooling to American production cars. The intercooler decreased the fuel/air mix temperature from the turbo-compressed-and-heated 300 degrees Fahrenheit to a denser, more effective 175 degrees. Even with the extra plumbing, the entire power plant weighed 150 pounds less than the 5.0-liter V-8 that produced the same power. The weight distribution difference would definitely benefit handling.

"People that are into GT cars," Negstad explained, "just love the SVO; it's fun to drive, qui-

et, directional stability is outstanding, it does all the good stuff. But for people who measure whether a car is good or bad with a stop watch. . . The first half a car length, a V-8 will beat it. Now after one car length, the SVO will stay with any V-8, but first car length it won't.

"We studied why this happened. Come to find out, the V-8 has a heavier flywheel. So we took an SVO and put a heavy flywheel on it. It would come out of the hole just like a V-8. However, it wouldn't pick up speed as well in midrange because it had to turn the bigger flywheel. It came down to another decision: Do you want a car to burn rubber or do you want to have a car that feels good at the top end?"

Ford already had a car to burn rubber. It was already called a Mustang, a 5.0 liter H.O. There was no need to have two.

Negstad retired from Ford in July 1988. He works now as a consultant engineer, solving other people's problems in his basement crammed with file cabinets and bookshelves floor to ceiling, sagging under the weight of documents, engineering books, computer data-run printouts, and other research. The engineering materiel contrasts with memorabilia from more than three decades of making Ford products, and those powered by Ford, handle well and go fast. A pile of photos of the SVO Mustang was nearby.

"When you do a car, you've got a million decisions to make on how you choose your compromises. You are literally able to create the vehicle like a canvas, drawing with paint. You must decide whether it's to be a landscape or a portrait. . . if you're gonna use perspective, is it single point or double point? Will it be futuristic or realistic or impressionistic? The same thing's true with a car, you have to decide what you're trying to achieve."

The rarer model of an already rare car was the code 41C, the models with the competition "delete radio" option. While this deleted the radio, it also took off the power door locks, power windows, and the air conditioning with its heavy compressor and additional plumbing, saving nearly 100 pounds (and crediting the buyer with $1,253) over the standard SVO. There were, however, no engine modifications.

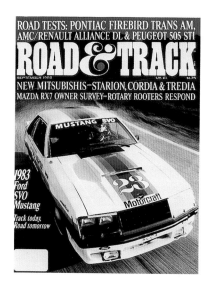

Cover proof of *Road & Track* September 1982 issue with inside story relating to the technical features of SVO's new race car. *Bob Negstad archives*

The million decisions included everything from seats to shocks to shifters. Each change from stock Mustang or even the Mustang GT would be one more element that would make the SVO into something different. And most all of them represented lesser or greater obstacles to be hurdled by the small group of dedicated people.

The first series of hurdles involved determining whether or not there actually would be a car. As early as January 1981, the SVO vehicle planning manager John Plant set out targets and objectives in a paper that read more like a magazine daydream of its automotive fantasy than a document to define terms to engineers. Two months later, in March 1981, Lyall and Negstad had worked out program assumptions—the cataloging of parts that would carry over from production Mustangs or other Ford products and those that would be new—for a car called the 1982-1/2 SVO Special Mustang. Then the base production Mustang was killed. Temporarily. But by the time it was back, SVO had put on hold all the papers for 1982-1/2 programs. And several months had passed. Now the Special Mustang would be a fall 1983 introduction for 1984 model year.

Production was set at a maximum of 10,000 cars for its first year. This small run created problems itself. The shock-absorber plant turned out more shocks in a week than the SVOs would need for a year's production. Revalving shocks to meet the performance characteristics that the engineers felt was essential was far too small a quantity for the regular supplier to accommodate. Koni, the Dutch company that had not been Ford suppliers since the early days of Shelby Mustangs, was glad to provide as *large* a quantity as required.

The rack and pinion steering system and hydraulic controls were sourced from TRW. Ford's Purchasing department had been trying to use in-house rack-and-pinions because TRW's assemblies cost more than anyone else's. But TRW was willing to adjust its hydraulic valving to create the on-center feel that SVO wanted for its Mustang.

Clutches that Ford Division used for its four-cylinder light trucks and passenger cars were not strong enough to handle the torque that SVO's engineers were getting out of the intercooled 2.3 liter engine. Dyken produced a clutch that would do the job.

"Tires," Bob Negstad laughed. "Came time for tires. I wanted a 16-inch tire. Chevrolet was fooling around with the Corvette with their Gatorbacks. Goodyear had a deal with [GM vice president of Styling Chuck] Jordan and it was a proprietary design, end of deal. So we found the NCT European tire for the Porsche 928 that was also Goodyear but was not a proprietary tread design. We cut a deal to use the NCT—although, because it was designed and developed for the Porsche, it wasn't quite as good a tire as a purpose-built Gatorback—it still got us tooled and running with our 16-inch wheels. And then when it came time to develop a tire for the SVO, Goodyear did a nice Gatorback for the Ford. We looked at seventeens at that point but it was more reach than we were willing to take."

Dearborn Assembly Plant had no facility to mount and balance SVO's new 16-inch tires. Micropoise Company developed an automatic machine to do the entire task. (When the SVO went out of production, it left behind the machinery in DAP, and it has been used since for the subsequent 16 and 17-inch tire and wheel combinations.)

"And styling, oh gosh, exterior styling." Negstad was running now, recalling in a steady stream all the struggles of producing an entire automobile with only thirty people, with final decisions coming from not more than a dozen of them. He alternated between laughter and somber head-shaking reminiscence.

"Our styling guys wanted to take the center of the hood—between where the headlights are—and have it droop down in the middle. And we needed a scoop in the hood for the intercooler. Well, 'Mainstream' seemed bound and determined they were not going to participate, they wanted mega dollars to do anything and we didn't have mega dollars. A tooled hood—inner and outer—through 'Mainstream' for a production car is $10 million. We only had $7 million to do the whole car.

"Mainstream didn't want to do the hood droop. They said, 'When you slam the hood, it vibrates, it would go down on 'over-slam' and chip the paint.' They had a little test that said you need to be able to drop the hood from its full height under its own weight and it has to stop on the bumpers. It can't go down and chip the paint. So they'd go out and get someone big to grab hold of the hood and just slam it down as hard as possible. It would chip a piece of paint and they'd write a 'Can't make,' 'Not acceptable for production, too many dings and dents for paint chips.' 'Get it outta here!'

"So Bob Stone and Lou Talamonti added some internal structure and put another couple bumpers on to support it on over-slam. And they tried it again and they couldn't hurt it. When we won that battle, we said, 'Okay, what's next?'" This was a moment for a Negstad laugh.

"'Oh. . . You really want to put this car in production. . .'"

"'That's right,' we said, 'and we're prepared to do whatever it takes.' And then they started coming around. Things got easier."

Well, not quite everything.

"The SVO Mustang had to have four-wheel disc brakes. Didn't need four-wheel disc brakes; you couldn't tell the difference in braking distance with cold four-wheel disc brakes. But it had to have them . . . They were there for high-performance [show room stock] fade resistance. But to do that was extremely complicated."

Now Negstad scowled.

"It's a three-ring circus putting disc brakes on the back of a drum-brake car. But we *had* to put disc brakes on the back of the Lincoln Versailles—the high-series Fox sedan—to help stop the car and pass our tests. So I adapted the brakes and axles out of the heavier Lincoln into the SVO. Front and rear.

"Why don't you have four-wheel disc brakes in all cars? Simple, you can't." The scowl deepened. "No, 'can't' is too strong a word. It is very, very, very, very difficult to make an emergency brake with disc brakes. Difficult. Very difficult. And costly.

"There are federal motor-vehicle safety standards on emergency brakes. And the tough one, the one that really bites ya, is that you have to go out and run the car and get all the brakes very hot, you go through fade tests. The car brakes are just smokin'.

"And then you put the car up on a 17 percent grade and you pull the emergency brake to the click that *just* holds it there. Shut off the engine and wait thirty minutes. Now as the brake

system cools off, it loses its grip and the car rolls back down the hill. And it fails the test.

"With a drum brake, as it cools it tightens up. Piece of cake. With a disc brake, although you get a lot of advantages, hill-holding is not one of them. So we had to have a system that dissipated the heat and didn't let the rotor in the hat section of the caliper get too hot so that it would hold on the hill. To do that, you have to put on a bigger and bigger brake rotor on the rear. You don't need it for stopping but you need it for hill holding."

Its most controversial feature was its twin-deck—or bi-plane—spoiler. Some within Special Vehicles Operations felt it was too distinctive and it ran the risk of being the single feature people would remember best if the car failed, like the exotic grille of the Edsel more than twenty-five years earlier. But in the end, the idea prevailed. It was functional too, sweeping rain and snow off the back window at speed.

To that end, the SVO Mustang used 11.1-inch-diameter discs on the front and 11.6-inch-diameter brakes on the rear.

"And adjusting the emergency-brake cables in the assembly plant? Tricky, and you can have your car spot-checked when it comes out of the plant by a federal inspector. If the assembly guys didn't do a good job adjusting the system, it fails and you got a recall and oh, man. . ."

A laugh.

"But we stuck with it, got it to work. Won another battle. Won three or four more battles. And the next ones got a little easier. And easier still. The engine guys did the same thing with their computer program for engine calibration. They developed a two-stage spark advance so someone could take the car into Mexico and not burn up the engine. Use lower-octane gasoline and not detonate, ping. And another part of the program controlled the turbo boost for the same reason." The computer would hold boost to 10 psi, 0.7 atmospheres below 2,500 rpm. Above that speed, boost would increase to 14 psi, one atmosphere. A switch on the dashboard manually limited it to 10psi to accommodate poorer gasoline.

In the middle of all this was another significant battle that Ford Motor Company was waging within itself. While Donald E. Petersen, who had been named president of Ford Motor Company, was a car enthusiast, his boss, Philip Caldwell was cost-conscious in the mold of Ernest Breech and Robert McNamara. Ford's middle-management ranks had grown fat with layers of decision-makers who worked harder to keep their jobs than to further efficient management and produce fine cars. A "blue-ribbon" panel had been created that had, among other goals, the task of determining just how low in the corporate hierarchy major decisions could be made. Buried in the project was the unuttered question: just how few people would it take to produce a car?

For each solution that the small group of dedicated people within SVO found, each battle that they won, the philosophy of the blue-ribbon committee was reinforced. Negstad remembered the benefits of trying to build a car that way.

"We were small enough that from my office to the engine guy was a divider and to the body guy was over the other divider and it was open at the top. And I could shout and get an answer, you know, like, 'Can I move the fuel line?'

"'Where you gonna move it to?'

'Well, I need to move it over here for wrench clearance.

"'Well, ask the engine guy.'

"'Hey, whadaya think? Does that bother you?'

"'No. I don't care about that. That's okay.'

"Done deal. In Mainstream, that decision could literally take months.

"We talked to each other, we were friends with each other. Everybody had a full plate and we had our staff meetings and discussed real problems. Where we needed help or where we could give ground and where we couldn't and why not. . ."

The entire car was made up of little things, the millions of decisions that Kranefuss and Lyall and engine wizard Dave Domine and marketing manager John Clinard and electronics genius Bob Stelmaszczak and the car's body fix-it man, Bob Stone, made on a daily—make that minute-to-minute—basis.

The gearshift knob could be sourced through 'Mainstream' for something like $.39. The thirty dedicated individuals afloat on the iceberg decided that they would spend money on a shifter that *felt good*, not just some plastic/vinyl ball that felt as though it came from an aftermarket auto parts accessory rack. The shift lever was formed around eppachlorhydron rubber (perchlor) formed inside a leather knob that was baseball stitched and embossed with the shift pattern on the top. Each one cost SVO a lot more than $.39.

Borg-Warner worked and reworked its T-5 transmission, finally achieving the feel that was necessary for a car that would go head-to-head against BMW's 3-series coupes. Hurst massaged and finessed its T-5 shift linkage with the same goal. But in fact, Borg-Warner and Hurst were made to understand that if they couldn't achieve the proper feel, Michael Kranefuss recalled a company in Germany, called Getrag, that probably could do what he wanted.

It was necessary, this coercion; these little differences were things the buyers would feel every time they took the car for a drive.

Color proofs of box covers produced by Monogram Models Inc., of the 1/24th scale model IMSA Miller Mustang and the Ford Motorsport Mustang in 1982. Monogram later did a 1/24th scale model of Ford's Mustang GTP race car. *Bob Negstad archives*

Ford's Back.

Get it together-buckle up.

Ford Motor Company is back in racing after ten years. Challenging the highly sophisticated European and American cars that compete on tracks across America, from Connecticut to California.

But we're not going racing like we did in the sixties. This is a small team with a small budget. And a small car. A specially prepared and modified Ford Mustang with a modified 4-cylinder Ford Fiesta engine.

Last season we won two races out of five, leading home 6 and 8-cylinder cars. Not through any outright power advantage, but through subtle, skillful engineering. For example, we used turbocharging and 4 valves per cylinder to produce a staggering 560 horsepower from the small 1.7 litre engine. Which gives the Mustang a top speed of 185 mph. And because we made the Mustang light and efficient, it was more nimble around the corners than its heavier competitors.

But highway drivers will benefit most from our return to racing. Because when you learn how to improve a car's performance on the track, you can apply that knowledge to improving your road cars as well. And that's exactly what we're doing. Next year's special high-performance turbocharged Ford Mustangs will feature refinements we learned in handling and engine performance. Such as the use of modified low pressure gas-filled shock absorbers, and the positioning of an intercooler between the turbocharger and the cylinder head, which significantly improves horsepower.

We are building these cars with you in mind. Because people want cars that provide all-round performance efficiently, cars that are fun to drive. Coming in first on the track is important. But using what we learn from racing to build better road cars for you is really where we're winning.

There's A Ford In America's Future.

Foot pedals *had* to be aligned for heel-and-toe pedaling during gear changes. A dead pedal *had* to be placed where the clutch foot rested naturally. Articulated, reclining supportive seats *had* to be used. Lear/Sigler seats provided better value for SVO's investment dollars than other accessory seat makers while providing all the comfort and support.

The fascia—the front piece of bodywork—was meant to accept aerodynamic, faired-in headlamps. Ford knew these were less than a year away from governmental legalization but until they were, standard flat-glass sealed beams had to be used. SVO's decision makers wanted the aero look but could not afford retooling a big complex piece after only a few thousand cars. Fabricating a fascia that would accept both styles of lamps along with its innovative below-the-bumper air intakes and fog-lamp mounts that incorporated federally mandated safety bumpers was a huge chore. Body engineer John Rundels called an old friend, Bob Stone, out of retirement. Stone had

Page proof of the actual "win ad" using the "Ford's back" headline. *Bob Negstad archives*

done chassis work on the '64-1/2 Mustang and before that he had worked on the Falcon and the vast sheet-metal surfaces of the big cars of the 1950s. He had friends far and wide within Body Engineering. Stone came in, looked at what was done so far and threw it away. Then he went to his friends, they pulled a few strings and yet another small group of dedicated people produced "grille-less" front fascia that would accept both types of headlights, bounce off barriers at 5 miles-per-hour and allow the engine to cool.

And then there was the bi-plane rear wing. A drag racer from the 1960s named Al Turner was involved in the grassroots racing promotions that SVO was doing as part of Ford Motorsports efforts. Turner had spent time in Europe and Australia for Ford and was familiar with Ford of Europe's Sierra XR-4i sports coupe series that wore a distinctive two-level rear spoiler. He recommended it and pushed hard for its adoption to the Mustang. Marketing manager John Clinard and others—older staffers within SVO who had

the same time as the regular 1984 product introductions. The SVO Mustang became a mid-1984 introduction, arriving in dealerships in mid-April in keeping with Mustang's entire history. However, even in pre-production assembly, just prior to Job One, there were more storm-tossed seas threatening the iceberg, more battles to challenge the small group's patience.

"The SVO Mustang went down the assembly line," Bob Negstad recalled. "And at Start-Up, it had, I think, some twenty-odd 'can't makes.' Those are plant problems that Automotive Assembly Division (AAD) writes up when the first cars go through the plant. Everybody finds something that they can't do, like their air hose isn't long enough to tighten that bolt. So that's a 'can't make.'

"We sat down in AAD's mahogany office and they read out the 'can't makes.' We resolved all of them—everyone of them—at the first meeting on the second day. We finished by 4 p.m. And the plant manager looked at us and said, 'You mean that's all the can't-makes on this car?'

"'Yeah. That means we *can make* it.' And we all got smiles on our faces because everybody had expected that this little dinky group of people were not going to bring a product down there without screwing up six ways to breakfast."

Negstad laughed hard.

The Mustang began production in the Dearborn Assembly Plant early in 1984. Almost immediately, one worker after another along the assembly line began taking on themselves the small additional tasks that would make the car "right." Bryce Russell produced a couple of boxes of baseball caps for SVO's Allen Park offices, and as the engineers patrolled the plant, watching out for problems, they noticed these successes. They started rewarding assembly-line workers with the SVO caps. This generated its own kind of friendly rivalry. First, everyone wanted one; then no one wanted to be known as the SVO worker who didn't earn one. The hats became highly prized along the SVO line within DAP and some of the workers assembling other cars displayed outright lust.

Through the next two years, the reputation of the SVO Mustang for quality became and remained solid, due in large part to the cap-wearers at DAP. SVO's collection of managers working

witnessed the distinctive grille of the Edsel—warned Turner that high-visibility features can hurt a car as much as help. Toned down from the Sierra (on which the top wing was aligned level with the roof line), it was finally agreed that it probably did fit the GT image even though it would never be appropriate for the tire-squealers.

Ford Division's late decision to carry over the Mustang delayed SVO in getting started. But the dozen key decision makers within SVO chose to delay it further, so that it would not arrive at

Ford's Mustang IMSA GTP (Grand Touring Prototype class) car sweeping through Laguna Seca's turn 7. It was built and campaigned by Ford's Special Vehicle Operations as part of Ford Motorsports. It used a 2.1-liter version of the in-line four-cylinder engine, turbocharged and intercooled.

Never have so few done so much for the enthusiast.

The enthusiast. It takes one to know one. That's why the 30 men at Ford Special Vehicle Operations are more than just engineers. Or technical experts. They're enthusiasts. That's what SVO is all about.

About power.
To get 175* horsepower and 210 lb/ft of torque from a 2.3 liter, 4-cylinder engine takes skill. And electronic fuel injection. Turbocharging. Forged aluminum pistons. High temperature alloy valves. A rev-limiter. And an air-to-air intercooler. Enthusiasts like power.

About precision.
It takes more than power to make an enthusiast happy. It takes the crisp feel of a Hurst® linkage on the 5-speed gearbox. It takes repositioned pedals that allow smooth heel-and-toe downshifting. And it takes the calculating brain of an electronic turbo boost con-trol to adjust boost, timing and air charge. Enthusiasts like precision.

About handling.
Mustang SVO knows how to handle itself. Adjustable Koni® gas-filled shocks on a Quadra-Shock performance suspension give you flexible control. A Traction-Lok rear axle with a 3.73:1 drive ratio

has a mean streak. It bites when cornered. Below, on 16x7 alloy wheels, unidirectional Goodyear Gatorback high-performance tires. The same tires that broke the 95-g barrier in skidpad tests and for fade-resistant stop-ping, power disc brakes on all four wheels. Enthusiasts like performance.

About value.
The SVO is so completely equipped, you only need to make three decisions. Yes or no to leather seats and a sunroof. And which color. But, because production of the SVO is limited, you need to make your decisions quickly. When they're gone, they're gone. Mustang SVO. What the enthusiast wants, the enthusiast gets.

*hp @ 60 SAE standard (1.6)

Have you driven a Ford... lately? *Ford*

Ford SVO

Get it together—Buckle up.

Color proof of double-page advertisement for the SVO Mustang, produced by J. Walter Thompson. *Bob Negstad archives*

out of their small headquarters, the Whitaker Building on Southfield Road in Allen Park, had put their effort—and their limited budget—into obvious performance and subtle appearance. Ironically, while reviewers noticed and noted the features that SVO had spent money on, the car was criticized for its tame styling. This echoed similar objections that some enthusiasts had voiced for Carroll Shelby's early Mustangs. Money had been spent to make the car perform better without looking radically different.

Still others thought its handling was tame.

"In 1984-1/2, the Koni shocks and struts were externally adjustable so the owner could cus-tomize the ride and handling to suit the needs," Bob Negstad recalled. "A red-and-white brochure and a white plastic knob explaining the procedure was included in the glove box. We established the shock valving to have good road manners and to have an overall good feel. This position on the ad-justment was called 'CITY RIDE.' The other ad-justment positions were called—in increasing or-der of stiffness—'CROSS COUNTRY,' 'GT/AGGRESSIVE DRIVING,' and 'COMPETITION.' However, the shocks were installed on the SVO in the soft 'CITYRIDE' position. I took it in the neck for the car not handling because it seems that nobody ever found the brochure and probably lost the ad-justment knob."

(Outside SVO, as the 302-ci V-8 power increased and tires got wider, power hop and brake hop got worse. It became bad enough that Jim Kennedy and Jim Elenburg were challenged to find a solu-tion. The Vehicle Office did "package work"—drawings to find clearances between axle, tire and shock and wheelwell—for the project. SVO was work-ing with Koni to develop a high-pressure monotube shock absorber expressly for this application. However, the system took more time to weld brack-ets onto the axle and provide weldnuts on the structure than SVO had so an interim fix called "slapper bars" was released for 1984. By 1985, quad shocks were ready for the SVO and the "Mainstream" V-8s.)

(This quad-shock system, plus a 0.67-inch diameter rear anti-sway bar, helped cornering im-mensely and almost completely tamed rear-axle hop during hard acceleration.)

"So for '85," Negstad continued, "I had Koni ship the shocks pre-adjusted to the firmer 'CROSS COUN-TRY' position so it had some harshness, so it felt like it was firmer. And in '86 I hardened it again because peo-ple assumed that if you liked it, it wasn't good. . . You were supposed to pay a little punishment for this love affair of driving this car. It can't be that comfortable. And when people drove it with the harder valving, they sighed 'Oh, God, now you got it right!'

"If there had been another, I'd have made it firmer again. So much for brochures and knobs."

But, there wasn't another. Introduced with 175 horsepower, the 1984 1/2 SVO sold for $15,585. With Ford's Traction-Lok differential and final drive of 3.45:1, magazine testers accomplished 0 to 60 times of 7.5 seconds and standing-start quarter-miles in 15.5 seconds at 90 miles-per-hour. While total Mustang sales amounted to 131,762 cars, only 4,508 of them were the three-door, black-trimmed SVOs.

For 1985, the black body trim was replaced with charcoal gray. At mid-year, for the first anniversary of the car, more significant changes were introduced. Electronics master Bob Stelmaszczak and engine-builder Dave Domine improved mileage (now up to 21 miles-per-gallon city and 32 miles-per gallon highway) and the engine's manners and power. They increased the boost from 14psi to 15, and Domine revised the intake manifold and the fuel-injection nozzles, increasing injection pump pressure; he replaced the cam and exchanged the air-to-air intercooler with one cooled by water. SVO engineers replumbed most of the exhaust system, splitting it into an honest dual-exhaust system aft of the single catalytic converter; this reduced back pressure by half. As a result of all this, output increased substantially, by 30 horsepower to 205 horsepower. The recessed sealed beam headlights were replaced with flush-mounted halogen lights that made negligible difference in the car's 0.38 coefficient of drag but great difference in visual appeal. Goodyear's P225/60VR16 Gatorbacks and a new rear-axle ratio (3.73:1, introduced at the beginning of the model year) shortened quarter-mile times by nearly half a second and raised trap speed more than 4 miles-per-hour. And steering response was quickened as its ratio was changed to 15:1 from 20:1 for the 85 cars. The price, remarkably, dropped to $14,806. Sales, even more remarkably, dropped precipitously, to only 1,954 cars. For 1986, there were no major changes to the car although the reality of lower-octane gasoline required reprogramming the EEC-IV module; this decreased the power rating to 200 horsepower. The suggested list price bounced back up to $15,272, but as word of mouth began to spread favorable conclusions, sales inched up to 3,382.

But 1986 was the final year. The decision to kill the Mustang was bouncing around once again in late 1983. The Mazda-built Probe had better EPA numbers that would make meeting Ford's CAFE requirements easier. Performance packages were also improving that car's image. It was selling well. Kranefuss and Lyall were informed that the Mustang would be dropped at the end of 1986. So the group of dedicated engineers, designers, thinkers, dreamers, and problem solvers asked for a Thunderbird. They could be perfectly content, they decided, tackling a new challenge. Oh yeah?, the Design Center and "Mainstream" responded. Well, how about a really dramatic looking car with a much lower cowl? Maybe a rear-engine two-seater, maybe a mid-engine? Perhaps all-wheel-drive? Harold "Red" Poling, head of North American Automotive Operations, himself, was funding it.

As work began on the aero-SVO T-Bird and the mid-engine sports car, the strength in the numbers of the United Auto Workers spoke to Ford. If you replace the Mustang with a car built outside of the U.S., they told Ford management, a great number of Dearborn workers may not have jobs. Their brothers and sisters in the unions working at other Ford plants around the U.S. might not take kindly to this. There might be some rough times. Soon Ford recognized that it could not afford to *not* retain the Mustang. It signed an agreement with the UAW to keep Mustang production in Dearborn at least through the 1993 model year.

A young engineer, Ron Muccioli, was transferred into SVO as it lined up its new projects. He struggled as hard as possible to make the mid-en-

Leather was an additional option to upgrade the interior of the SVO. But as intriguing as the few options available to add to the SVO was the option that deleted equipment. Called "comp prep," designating "race" use, it was not offered in 1984-1/2. Production was limited to forty models for 1985, and in 1986 only eighty-three were built. The SVO introduced European-type road-holding and performance to a reluctant American audience.

Another unique feature to the exterior styling of the SVO Mustang was its "drooped" nose that incorporated no grille. All cooling air hit the radiators from openings below the front bumper. The SVO Mustang perfected the four-bar link rear suspension system, the first arrangement to effectively tame wheel hop in acceleration as well as greatly improve cornering and road-holding.

gined two-seater cost effective enough to build. In the end, it couldn't make the right numbers against another product, a proposed sports utility vehicle. With only enough development money available to Ford Division to complete one of the two projects, priorities were set: The Explorer went into production; the sports car did not. Ron already had experience with priorities, however; his mother Anna had discussed them with Henry Ford II and Lee Iacocca during a shareholders meeting back in 1968.

In its two-and-a-half model years, only 9,842 SVO Mustangs were sold, less than the first-year target of 10,000 copies. But it was conceived as a low-volume image builder, and it exceeded its break-even point of 8,500 cars in total. The SVO Mustang was meant to set a benchmark for what was possible from Ford using a small, fuel-efficient four-cylinder engine. It was meant to express Ford's commitment to those engines as a power plant for the future.

The SVO Mustang did establish several things. Magazines referred to it as the "best handling, most balanced Mustang ever sold." But it never got those kind of raves from European reviewers who came over to drive it. Even though it was so well equipped that it only offered six options—air conditioning, power windows, power door locks, leather seats, flip-up sunroof and AM/FM stereo cassette radio—it never drew into the showrooms any of the 3-series BMW owners that SVO hoped would materialize. Worse, the American car buyers who went in, ready to buy one were regularly talked into a GT by dealership personnel who just didn't understand the car. The GT, with its 5.0 liter H.O. didn't have to wait for the turbos to wind up for its identical 200 horsepower to arrive. And buyers didn't have to spend an additional $4,170 to get it. In the end, it was defeated by its own stablemates as much as any other car on the market.

On top of that, the racing Mustang GTP disappointed all who bet on it. The Ford Motorsports high-performance street and racing parts supply and the racing operations remained under SVO control. However, by 1988 all Mustang manufacture was taken back inside Ford Division. Only two prototype mid-engine cars were built, and only five or six of the prototype SVO Thunderbirds were built before the cool, efficient, but much smaller iceberg was cast adrift once more.

14

Faithful Fox
1986–1993

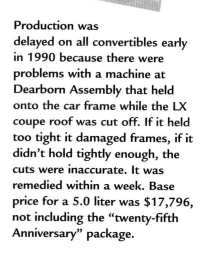

As SVO struggled to reinvent the wheel, as it tried to educate American car buyers as to what a performance car could be, most of those buyers looked at its price and its engine and said, "No thanks, I'd rather have a V-8."

Buyers took not only the V-8, they also took the 3.8-liter V-6 and even the normally aspirated 2.3-liter four more often than the high-tech, turbocharged, and intercooled SVO. It was the high price for high performance from the small engine that never caught the Ford Mustang customer's imaginations. While the 2.3-liter, one-barrel carbureted, standard engine retained its 88 horsepower (the Turbo GT was dropped after only one year, in 1985), the 3.8 liter held at 120 horsepower, and it was the standard engine with the LX convertible package. It was a potent enough mix for buyers interested in enough power to enter the freeways but not interested in the high insurance rates or higher fuel consumption of the 5.0 liter and the GT package.

But SVO tricks bled through. In 1985, the 5.0 got real dual exhausts and, ahead of the catalytic converter, the big V-8 got real 1960s-era stainless-steel tube headers. With a longer duration cam and hydraulic roller valve lifters (to reduce friction and help CAFE), power output increased to 210 horsepower. The base 2.3-liter two-door sedan was listed at $6,989 while the LX convertible was priced at $12,237. The 5.0-liter three-door GT sedan was $10,224, and the convertible was $13,930. The five-speed overdrive transmission that was standard on the GT cost $124 as an option for the LX, but a SelectShift three-speed automatic transmission was standard on the LX convertible. Air conditioning was $762, the T-roof was $1,100, and leather articulated sports seats could be added to the LX convertible for $780 or to the GT convertible for $415.

Magazine testers loved the 5.0-liter GT three-door with its four-barrel carburetor. They made great photographs for the covers, their back-ends enveloped in tire smoke. Reviewers obtained 0 to 60 mile per hour times of 7.1 seconds and quarter-mile times of 15.5 seconds at 89.7 miles per hour. The 3,000-pound car would average 17 miles per gallon under their mixed (make that *hard*) use. Ford produced 156,514 Mustangs in 1985.

Road & Track magazine published a comparison of Ford's 1986 GT and Chevrolet's IROC-Z. The results must have sold a lot of Mustangs because in each acceleration measure, 0 to 30, 0 to 60, and 0 to 100 miles per hour, the Mustang arrived a full second ahead of the Camaro. While fuel-economy figures were nearly identical, fully equipped costs differed by about $3,500 to the Mustang's advantage. The only test where the Camaro out-performed the GT was on the skid pad where the Camaro cornered at 0.845g and the GT made only 0.792, a fact that *R&T* attributed to wider, fatter Goodyear Eagle P245/50VR-16s on the Camaro while the GT wore sixty-series tires, Goodyear Eagle P225/60VR-15s. But through the slalom, the Mustang ran 60.9 miles per hour while the Camaro only made 59.7 miles per hour. The Mustang weighed 240 pounds less, at 3,355 pounds, and produced 20 horsepower more, at 210.

The two-door LX sedan with a standard 2.3-liter four was up to $7,420 for 1986. The LX convertible, still with the 3.8-liter V-6, was still at 120 horsepower, and had increased to $13,214, and the 5.0-liter GT convertible was up to $14,945. Those Goodyear VR60s cost an additional $674

Production was delayed on all convertibles early in 1990 because there were problems with a machine at Dearborn Assembly that held onto the car frame while the LX coupe roof was cut off. If it held too tight it damaged frames, if it didn't hold tightly enough, the cuts were inaccurate. It was remedied within a week. Base price for a 5.0 liter was $17,796, not including the "twenty-fifth Anniversary" package.

Opposite
1990 Limited Edition Mustang 5.0-liter LX convertible
It was available only Emerald Jewel Green clearcoat metallic, with Oxford white interior including white leather seats and a white convertible top. All of these, something like 4,103, were built at the Dearborn Assembly Plant. Production began in December 1989; however, the plant didn't reach full speed until February 2, and assembly continued through May 29, 1990.

LX convertibles started life as coupes. The hardtops were removed, and the cars were shipped to Cars & Concepts, Brighton, Michigan, to have the convertible top and the retracting mechanisms installed. These Limited Edition cars were sold either with a four-speed, automatic, overdrive transmission or a Borg-Warner T-5 manual. Ford included a driver's air bag.

with alloy wheels; the T-roof was up only $20, to $1,120, and the leather seats were unchanged. Production climbed to 224,410.

There were big changes for 1987. Most noticeable was that the tenth edition of the Fox platform was given a pretty thorough face-lift, especially in the GT package. The drooped nose of the SVO was adopted; all the Mustangs became "bottom breathers," that is, their major radiator air access came from below the bumper belt line. The aero-headlamps with halogen bulbs were carried over from the SVO and so was the major handling improvement of the SVOs quad-shock rear-axle suspension, fitted standard to the GTs. As if that wasn't enough, Ford electronic fuel injection (EFI) that was introduced during the 1986 model run (and offered 210 horsepower out of the 5.0-

liter engine) was now perfected with the 5.0 liter High Output and horsepower surged to 225. The 3.8-liter V-6 was dropped so only the base 2.3-liter single-barrel and the EFI H.O. remained.

The five-speed manual transmission was made standard on all models, its low final overdrive gear benefiting mileage figures. In reality, only the LX convertible suffered most notably from the loss of the 3.8-liter V-6. Its standard engine now was the 2.3 liter. The two-door LX sedan sold for $8,271, the LX convertible was now $13,052, while the GT convertible broke into the realm previously occupied only by the SVO. It was listed at $15,852. The automatic overdrive transmission was a $515 option to either LX or GT models; the T-roof cost $1,618 for the GT and $180 more—$1,798—for the LX. The price of cowhide was unchanged, remaining at $780 for leather seats on the LX convertible, $415 for the GT rag tops.

Road & Track revisited its comparison of the Mustang GT and the Camaro IROC-Z, tackling both 1987 models in its October 1986 issue. The IROC-Z was up to 220 horsepower while the GT, of course, produced 225 horses. The weight spread was nearly the same as the year before, at 3,720 pounds for the Camaro, and 3,500 for the GT. Final drive ratios, 3.27 for the Chevy, and 3.08:1 for the Ford, remained unchanged as did tire sizes. But Chevrolet made good use of its extra thirty horses under the hood.

Times for acceleration were now within tenths, the GT winning the 0 to 60 miles per hour contest by one-tenth at 6.7 seconds versus the Camaro's 6.8. But going on to 100 miles per hour, the Camaro's sleeker shape gave it a four-tenths advantage, getting there in 18.4 seconds compared to 18.8 for the GT. Fatter tires got the Camaro around the oval at a higher G-load, but more nimble handling got the GT through the slalom at 63.6 miles per hour compared to 63.3 miles per hour for the Camaro. Both cars even came within one mile per hour of top speeds—149 for the Camaro, 148 for the Mustang. (During the *R&T* test, Ford's Product Development Engineer Arch Cothran let slip that the car was even faster in fourth gear than fifth. But the development engine gave up before the testers did, almost at redline in fourth, approaching 149 miles per hour.) The only dramatic differential was in price, where once again the smart money put $1,350 back in its pocket and bought the GT. (The Camaro was base priced at $12,675 while the GT listed at $11,324.)

The GT also had several distinctive appearance features lacking on the LX, including multilouvered taillights and front and rear air dams as well as a side-aerodynamic valence with scoops to front and rear brakes. Inside, "tasteful functionalism" were the appearance watchwords. The interior was designed by Englishman Trevor Creed who had earlier designed the interior of Ford of Europe's Scorpio (imported by Lincoln-Mercury as the Merkur) and then the interiors for the Taurus and Thunderbird.

Road & Track's reviewers captured the essential differences between the Mustang and the Camaro and in brief comments summed up Ford's approach: "It was easy to hop into one and just *know* it was the grandest car on the road. The Mustang did this with its nimble, fighter-like response and sudden bursts of acceleration. In convenience and utility the Mustang offers advantages." Elsewhere, it characterized the comparison between ride and handling: "Ford chose ride quality; Chevy chose handling ability."

In 1987, Ford chose to build 159,145 of the cars. Nomenclature changed with the body styles. Gone were the three-door sedans, replaced by two-door hatchbacks.

The specter of a Japanese-based Mustang reared its head once again in 1987. Again, the UAW's impressive force was felt, and the proposal moved off Mustang drawing boards and styling tables and out to Flat Rock, Michigan, for production—as the 1988 Probe.

Writer Mel Nichols, reporting in *Automobile*, likened the new 5.0-liter GT hatchback with its 302 cubic-inch displacement to the 302s of seventeen and eighteen years earlier. In 1970, 0 to 60 miles per hour came in 6.0 seconds; in 1987, it was 6.1 in his tests. In 1970, the top speed was 118, in Nichols experience it was 145 miles per

The 5.0-liter 90-degree V-8 was rated at 225 horsepower for 1990. Throttle-body electronic fuel injection handled mixing chores. Automatic transmission cars outnumbered those sold with the five-speed manuals, 2,743 to 1,360. For owners looking for even more performance, Steve Saleen provided an aftermarket supercharger installation, and at least a dozen cars were built this way.

The white leather seats were electrically and manually adjustable. Lower back lumbar support and side bolsters operated electrically. The front cushion below the thighs pulled out for three manual adjustments for comfort. Power windows and door locks were part of the "Special Value Package #245" that also included air conditioning, an AM/FM premium sound system, and speed control.

hour. He quoted photographer Tim Wren at the end of a hard drive: "'It doesn't have the grace and refinement of a good European car this fast,' he said, and started to grin. 'But at the end of the day you have to say, Damn—that was fun!'"

For 1988, it was better yet. *Road & Track* headlined their profile of the GT in their *1988 Performance Cars Special*, quoting a lyric from singer Carly Simon, "Stay right here,' 'cause these are the good old days."

To remember back to the recent bad days—the dark ages induced by OPEC, to September 1974 when Henry Ford II showed Anna Muccioli a little jewel with a white vinyl roof and Ford's first new four-cylinder engine since the 1930s—then to recall the glory days—the Hi-Po K-codes of 1966, the Cobra Jet Drag Pack SportsRoofs of 1969, the Boss 429 of 1970—it could only seem as though this were a renaissance. The dark ages had ended, and the lights had come back on, both in Dearborn and in the eyes of the behold-

ers, buyers for the 211,225 Mustangs Ford would produce in 1988.

And that, as *Road & Track 1988 Performance Cars* writer John Katz put it, is what it was all about. "Ford Motor Company," he wrote, "like any automaker, is in business to sell cars, not history." But if it happened to make a little history each year, that wasn't a bad thing. "The hatchback GT," he concluded, "offers a glorious trip back in time, with the windows rolled down, the stereo filling the atmosphere with rock 'n' roll, the exhaust shaking the asphalt with its thunder. It's the Mustang legend come alive, and you feel a part of it every time you take the wheel. Only the legend has never been more true, nor the Mustang ever better than it is right now."

The legend, in the body of the GT hatchback, sold for $12,745, the convertible—produced by Cars and Concepts, not in house at the Dearborn Assembly Plant—sold for $16,610 while the base 2.3-liter LX two-door was listed for $8,835. Air conditioning was $788, the T-roof was discontinued, and leather remained an inflation fighter, its price unchanged in three model years.

The next year, Ford chose to ignore the calendar. While it had proudly produced the Mustang II in the tenth anniversary year of the car's birth and while the 1984 GT350s were called Twentieth Anniversary Commemorative models, there was no twenty-fifth anniversary special edition in 1989. The official reason was that the company had begun to consider that the April introduction was really half a year early for the 1965 model—and it began referring to early and late 1965s instead of 1964-1/2 models. As had been the case between 1987 and 1988, there were virtually no significant changes once again between previous year and new model cars. Prices rose as expected. The base two-door LX sedan was now $9,050, the GT convertible was up to $17,001. Air conditioning was up, to $807, and at last, leather seats' price increased to $855 for the LX convertible (itself up to $14,140) and $489 for the GT convertible.

As the 1988 Probe was being readied for Job One, concern in Dearborn turned ever more acutely to the future of the Mustang. Ford had become convinced that a Japanese product, even if assembled completely in Michigan, but with-

out the one necessary ingredient—a V-8—would hurt not only Mustang sales but, in these latter days of President Ronald Reaganomics, a Japanese car would also hurt sales of all Ford products.

The idea of an SVO-type organization, small, streamlined, and highly efficient, was resurrected to conceive of the car that would replace the gracefully aging Fox. Stories in the newspapers began to reveal the history of a small, wildly creative, clandestine group of Lockheed aircraft engineers who had produced the remarkable U-2 and SR-71 surveillance aircraft and the nearly in-

visible Stealth bomber. Ford Mustang Program Manager Ken Dabrowski admired the idea.

Ford's group would ultimately call themselves Team Mustang, and they set out to conceive of a new Mustang while the company continued to produce barely changed models through 1989 and 1990. It produced 209,769 of them in 1989.

The two-door LX sedan was priced at $9,753 while the GT convertible required a savings withdrawal of $18,418. After fifteen years, Mustang speedometers could finally acknowledge that

These cars were promoted during the 1990 National Collegiate Athletic Association basketball finals. The 7-Up Bottling Co. was to give away thirty of these models during an audience participation contest. Anyone who sunk a basket from center court—one try per contestant—drove home in the new Mustang. But at the last minute the promotion was canceled.

there were speeds above 85 miles per hour; GT Mustangs and 5.0 liter-engined LXs, now called LX 5.0L Sports (in sedan, hatchback, and convertible) were all fitted with new speedometers marked to 140 miles per hour. Production of all Mustangs for 1990 slipped to just 128,189 cars. This included a 2,000-car production run of Emerald Green GT convertibles with white leather interior that Ford called the Limited Edition Twenty-Fifth Anniversary model. Basically an LX 5.0L convertible, it was listed for $19,878. It was so appealing and so successful that 3,837 were produced ultimately .

The U.S. economy was doing its own version of a brake fade test, stopping and starting and stopping again. It was proving to be not quite so fade resistant as the Mustang's brakes. For 1991, production fell again, this time to 98,737 cars. The prices had risen again slightly, but another financial milestone was passed when the base price of the LX two-door sedan was published at $10,157, with the 2.3-liter, overhead cam four now with twin-spark-plug ignition, multiport electronic fuel injection, five-speed manual transmission, power front disc and rear drum brakes, and P195/75R14 radial black sidewall tires as part of the standard equipment. The GT convertible was nearly double the cost, at $19,864, but was now running on 16-inch tires and wheels.

In 1992, the baseline two-door LX sold for $10,215 while the GT convertible was published at $20,199. For years the technical features, engineering features, and appearance of the Fox platform had remained largely unchanged. This, coupled with many years of Mustang buyers and performance car enthusiasts hearing and reading about the uncertain future of the car beyond 1993, caused sales to continue slipping. The success of the Limited Edition emerald green convertible sparked a new version for 1992, in vibrant red, but repeating the white convertible top and white leather seats of the 1990 car. It was an $850 option that 2,196 buyers selected. Production of all Mustang models in 1992 reached 79,280 cars.

For model year 1993, three Limited Edition cars were introduced: A yellow LX 5.0L convertible with white interior (1,419 produced) and a white on white convertible (1,460 produced) were available from the start of the year, and a new Cobra was introduced in 1993-1/2, with its 5.0-liter V-8 tweaked to produce 235 horsepower at a time when new SAE standards reduced the horsepower rating of the standard 5.0 to 205. As a premium-priced ($19,990) Limited Edition car, it was produced by Ford's Special Vehicles Team (SVT—which assumed SVO's car-producing responsibilities) with performance improvements invented and perfected by outside engine-modification magician Jack Roush. It was very popular, selling just seven cars shy of its projected production run: dealers moved 4,993 cars in half a model year.

Road & Track recorded 0 to 60 mile per hour times of 5.9 seconds and the quarter-mile slipped past in 14.5 seconds at 98.0 miles per hour. With its extremely tall fifth (overdrive) gear of 0.68:1, 2,000 rpm yielded 65 miles per hour, and highway economy was quoted as 24 miles per gallon, impressive for a car that could be driven less conscientiously to about 150 miles per hour. Despite huge 245/45ZR-17 Goodyear Eagles, the ride comfort was actually higher than standard GTs due to interesting blends of standard LX springs with stiffer-than-GT bushings.

While the 1993 Mustang Cobra carried its maturity well, it was clearly aging. The interior and the body (now boasting a very noticeable rear spoiler) had been around for fourteen years. But the car accomplished two goals. First, it made a statement to the enthusiast world: One was actually penned by *R&T* writer Douglas Kott, who characterized it as "the hardest-accelerating, quickest-stopping, best-handling pony car from Ford yet." Quality may be Job One but performance was clearly priority one.

This 1993-1/2 Cobra introduction accompanied news that there definitely would be a 1994 Mustang and that it would be a new car. So the other purpose that this limited edition, high-performance hatchback with its distinctive rear wing served was the same kind of hint that Lee Iacocca had dropped thirty years earlier: The Cobra was something "to show the kids that they should wait for us because we had some good, hot stuff coming."

The 5.0 liter H.O. incorporated Saleen-designed high-flow heads, cast upper and lower intake manifolds, and stainless-steel exhaust headers. A 70-millimeter Saleen mass airflow sensor worked with a 65-millimeter throttle body. Saleen/Ford SVO rocker arms were used. Power output was quoted as 225 horsepower at 4,000 rpm and 300 foot-pounds of torque at 3,200 rpm. Performance was 0 to 60 miles-per-hour in 6.2 seconds, with the quarter-mile taking 14.7 seconds. The strut tower brace was a unique Saleen piece.

Opposite
1990 Saleen Fastback
Steve Saleen's modified Mustangs were easy to recognize with their Autosport Aerodynamics package that included the competition-design rear spoiler, front air dam, side skirts, and rear valence. The Racecraft Suspension lowered the entire car about 1.5 inches. It included progressive-rate front and rear coil springs, Monroe Formula GP front struts, rear shocks, and rear-axle dampers on the Quadra-shock rear suspension. Saleens rode on General XP2000 225x50VR16 tires.

15

Into the Future at
140 Miles Per Hour

Random rules and regulations:

1. The program manager must be delegated practically complete control of his program in all aspects. He should have the authority to make quick decisions regarding technical, financial, or operational matters.

3. The number of people having any connection with the project must be restricted in an almost vicious manner. Use a small number of good people.

4. Very simple drawing and drawing release system with great flexibility for making changes must be provided in order to make schedule recovery in the face of failures.

7. The contractor must be delegated and must assume more than normal responsibility to get good vendor bids for subcontract on the project.

13. Access by outsiders to the project and its personnel must be strictly controlled.

These were not excerpts of rules posted outside Roy Lunn's project studio for Mustang I. Nor were they part of the sign on the door welcoming visitors to Special Vehicle Operations in Allen Park. Neither were they segments of the security release to be signed upon entering the old Montgomery Ward warehouse occupied by Team Mustang.

No, these were five of the fourteen basic operating rules that were quoted in Ben Rich's 1994 book, *Skunk Works*. This book related the inside story of Lockheed's top-secret Advanced Development Projects, and these principles were set out by founder Kelly Johnson during World War II when the department was established. "Skunk works" was the nickname of a cabin in Al Kapp's cartoon strip, "L'il Abner," from which all kinds of amazing and amusing inventions, potions,

and creations came to "skunk" the outsiders. Johnson's Skunk Works was Lockheed's version of "the small group of dedicated people." And in his book, Rich acknowledged it was the model for Team Mustang. (Its principles had been reflected and adopted unknowingly by Lunn and Kranefuss. With Kranefuss and Lunn—as with Johnson—it was just viewed as the most efficient way to get their jobs done.)

And so it was again in late 1988 when Mustang Program Manager Ken Dabrowski formed an ad hoc Skunk Works, composed of engineers, designers, marketing personnel, and product planners who had already begun formulating their own ideas for a Fox replacement. Something in the neighborhood of $1 billion would be anticipated to fund the new car from creation through development, testing, marketing, promotion, and manufacture. Mustang Engineering Design Manager John Coletti's proposal suggested that, with a dedicated Skunk Works team in its own off-campus facility, it might be possible to bring in a new car for perhaps half so large an investment. They had enough time to do a proper car—this was still four-and-a-half years before Job One—but in an age when money saved might be invested back into the product, this was a significant, adaptive re-use of the experiences gained by the SVO staff. But this, of course, was meant to be a much bigger program, selling many more cars per month than SVO sold per year.

It would take nearly another year, until the promotion of Alex Trotman to executive vice president of North American Automotive Operations, before the Skunk Works would be approved—by now, early August 1989. Trotman had

The 302-cubic-inch V-8 used sequential electronic fuel injection and cast-aluminum intake manifolds. With bore and stroke of 4.0x3.0 inches, the cast aluminum-alloy pistons fired into GT40-design cast-iron cylinder heads atop a cast-iron block. Output was 240 horsepower at 4,800 rpm with torque at 285 foot-pounds at 4,000 rpm.

Opposite
1994 Mustang Cobra coupe
Built on the new Fox-4 chassis, the 1994 Mustang was 181.5 inches long overall on a 101.3-inch wheelbase. Height was 53.4 inches, width was 71.8 inches, and the Cobra weighed 3,365 pounds. Transmission was the manual shift T-5 overdrive with limited slip differential and 3.08:1 final drive.

The body of the 1994 Mustang and the Mustang Cobra were designed by Bud Magaldi based largely on a styling studio concept that was nicknamed "Arnold Schwarzenegger." Within Ford Motor Company, the entire project was known as SN-95, referring to the fact that it was a specialty-type vehicle with planning supervision from North American Automotive Operations. It was approved in late October 1990.

been manager of Product Planning for Ford of Europe through the 1960s, and his experience with the German Capris and American Mustangs had convinced him of the necessity of investing in the project. The Skunk workers, who had begun laboring on a project on their own time after hours, now had company time for their efforts. In an engineers' version of Iacocca's Fairlane Committee dinners, the Skunk workers met at 4 p.m. on Thursdays in John Coletti's office in Ford's engineering building No. 3. Dinners were often ordered in. There were eight of them, just like Iacocca's Fairlane Committee. In charge was Coletti, aided by SVO-alumnus Ron Muccioli as product planning manager. Styling

and Design manager John Aiken was enlisted immediately to begin a full-size clay model, to look more Taurus-like than Fox-Mustang-like. They were joined by Mike Ferrence as sales and marketing manager, Bo Kovacinski as finance manager, and Joe Corvaia as purchasing manager. Body and assembly was represented by Dia Hothi, body and chassis engineering by Sid Wells, and the powertrain engineering manager was SVO graduate Tom Logar.

Together, they established a product description and program objectives. It was clear from Ford's union obligations and from a ground swell of negative public reaction about the Mazda Mustang that the car had to remain front-engined and rear-wheel driven; It had to offer a V-8 engine, in addition to whatever baseline power plant was selected. It needed to look entirely different inside and out, it had to conform to all the expected governmental safety and environmental regulations; its build quality needed to be improved substantially; and it had to continue to be offered as both coupe and convertible.

While Styling and Design Manager John Aiken worked with a hastily assembled team, including designers Dave Rees, John Doughty, and Mark Conforzi, to produce a full-size idea of what the car could look like, Coletti sent Bo Kovacinski, Joe Corvaia, and their groups off to meet with all the outside vendors to determine ways to obtain better products and still cut costs by as much as 25 percent.

By June 1990, two separate body styles created around the same specifications—hard points—were completed, one by Aiken and his colleagues, the other by Ford's West Coast design shop, the Hutting Design Center in Valencia, California. At a design clinic in June 1990 held in Pomona, California, the Valencia car was judged to be too mild visually while the audience made it clear that even the Dearborn car could go farther.

The silver Dearborn prototype was nicknamed "Bruce Jenner" because it was lean and clean-cut but muscular in the athletic way that former Olympic decathlon winner and sometimes racing driver Jenner was when he won his gold. But Aiken encouraged Rees and Doughty to free their imaginations. They created an evil, dark-hearted cousin, also in silver, but with lines that dipped where Jenner's lines remained horizontal. Nicknamed "Rambo," it provoked immediate responses from people who thought it went too far. But from Rambo and Jenner was born the car nicknamed "Arnold Schwarzenegger," a Jenner that got "pumped" up. It became *the* design, and quickly two driveable prototypes were created.

The chassis would be a heavily modified Fox monocoque that was different enough to be renamed Fox-4. Bob Negstad, retired by this time, was hired back to consult, and he recommended chassis changes to improve steering and stability. The Skunk Works team produced one chassis

prototype with Negstad's changes and a second with slightly less modification. Following several evaluations, in May 1990 Ford Automotive Group President Allan Gilmour asked to see the car. He ended up taking the slightly changed prototype for a vigorous drive around Dearborn's tight handling course and was impressed. Gilmour recommended showing the car to Harold Poling, Ford's chairman of the board who was also pleased with the progress, all of which had been accomplished outside of regular working hours and in addition to normal responsibilities.

At that point, Coletti returned to Alex Trotman and suggested they continue on the same way—with very little funding—until a final design clinic in San Jose, California, in October 1990 at which Jenner, Rambo, and Schwarzenegger would be shown. When the audience overwhelmingly preferred "Arnold," the decision was set. Management on either side of Trotman concurred. The 1994 Mustang Program was approved, and Job One was set for December 1993.

The Skunk Works team was officially dissolved, their job done. In fact, nearly all of them joined "Team Mustang" working on a project internally named SN-95, a code sequence to track prototype and pre-production status of the project that was defined as Specialty vehicle (S) with primary design responsibility handled by North American Automotive Operations (N) .

Prior to this, but certain of approval, the Mustang Skunk Works knew it would need a home to finish the car. Coletti's proposal of a staff, free from other assignments, working under one roof together off-campus, was sure to be accepted as well; his choice of personnel had already proven itself on this project. Something in the neighborhood of 45,000 square feet were estimated to house operations as diverse as design, finance, marketing, and styling, and for building, modifying, and repairing prototypes. Space was located in a recently converted Montgomery Ward warehouse on Southfield Road in Allen Park, not far from SVO's home. Conveniently, Jack Roush had facilities in what had become a high-tech complex, and Roush already was slated to assist in the mechanical and engineering prototype creation. In August 1990, the design team moved into Suite 600 in the complex. By the

October program approval, work was already underway on the cars, and renovation of the raw warehouse space had been nearly completed as offices, studios, and garages.

Wheelbase of the Fox-4 grew 0.8 inches to 101.3 inches while front and rear track bulged 1.9 inches on the GTs, to 60.6 inches front and 59.1 inches rear. Four-wheel disc brakes used 10.8-inch discs front and 10.5-inch rotors in the rear, with Bosch's ABS2U anti-lock braking system offered as an option on both the GT and the base model car, now fitted with a new 3.8-liter V-6. The 3.8 liter used a number of aluminum components, and as a result, while it produced 145 horsepower, it was nearly as light as the 2.3-liter in-line four that it replaced. The 5.0 liter H.O. was improved with better intake breathing, and output was up to 215 horsepower. Both engines were operated by the EEC-IV electronic engine management system, in place since 1987, but with updated programs for emissions requirements.

Ford offered its four-speed automatic-overdrive transmission for both engines while the five-speed Borg-Warner T-5 was standard. Traction-Lok was available.

Early on during discussions regarding the car's appearance, chassis engineering observed that it has always been difficult to maintain chassis rigidity with a three-door or a hatchback body style. As a result, Coletti and his Skunk workers decided from the start to produce only the coupe and convertible. The coupe's roof line was designed, however, based on the early product decision to make a detachable hardtop roof for the convertible; it would be ideal if it closely resembled the fixed roof line. (The finished top weighed 84 pounds, and was offered as a $2,000 option, finished with interior head liner and dome light. The roof line was just about impossible to differentiate from the coupe's from a distance.)

In May 1992, John Coletti learned that Chevrolet and Pontiac Divisions would introduce their new Camaro and Firebird to the public during the January 1993 Detroit and Los Angeles auto shows. The SN-95 was not due till a year after that, but with his competitive juices flowing, he wondered how to "skunk" GM. He recalled the show cars done in Mustang's early days to tantalize customers and frustrate competitors: Mustang I in 1962, Mach I in 1967, and Mach II, the wild mid-engine concept car in 1969. He conceived of a Mach III, but as an open car after the style of the Mustang I from thirty years before. To further skunk GM, this new car also had to be driveable, just like Mustang I.

Mach III project manager Joe Laura and Coletti sketched ideas, more akin to Rambo but even exaggerated beyond that. A 4.6-liter modular V-8 was selected because, first, it was a V-8, and second, it was Ford's newest high-tech showpiece engine. Advance Powertrain Engineering Chief Jim Gagliardi supercharged this version and fitted it with intake manifolds that were inter-cooled with ethylene glycol—essentially antifreeze—to reduce intake fuel-air mix temperatures by about 75 degrees. When it was all done, Ford claimed 450 horsepower and mated it to a six-speed Borg-Warner T-56 transmission. It was assembled by Masco-Tech, a concept- and show-car builder based in suburban Mt. Elliott, Michigan. Coletti's idea, Laura's shape, and Gagliardi's engine lured viewers away from GM. At the Los Angeles show, Ford and Pontiac shared the same hall, and the Mach III's vivid red paint grabbed and held onto show attendees before they ever saw Pontiac's deep-blue Trans Am.

The 1994 Mustang was introduced December 9, 1993, but as early as the May 1993 issue of *Road & Track*, their Detroit-based writer Ken Zino produced a seven-page comparison of the future Mustang and Camaro, featuring water-color illustrations of the two cars. Zino could draw no conclusions at this early date and conceded that there were too many unknowns to hazard a judgment. He would wait until the November issue to try the car and sum up his reactions:

"On first drive, there's no question that the 1994 Mustang is sufficiently improved to keep the Ford pony-car tradition growing for a few more years. Sporty, not radical, styling, good power, and a distinctively American rear-drive character are Mustang's attractions once again."

In *R&T's Sports & GT Cars* annual, author Tom Wilkinson compared Mustang's GT with Camaro's Z-28, both convertibles. With its fully optioned test price at $27,225 compared to Camaro's $25,852, and with Mustang's 5.0 liter producing 215 horsepower compared to Chevrolet's new environmentally corrected LT-1 (the new 5.7 liter replacing an older, dirty engine) cranking out 275 horsepower, it was easy to understand where the Mustang came up short—in performance and price. But Ford turned up the fire with its 240 horsepower 1994 Cobra, selected as pace car for the seventy-eighth Indianapolis 500, May 29, 1994. Three Jack Roush-prepared official pace cars, as well as another 105 non-Roush-modified convertibles for use by officials and Indianapolis 500 race VIPs, were assembled during the month. An additional 1,000 were manufactured as pace car replicas and sold for $24,010. An additional 250 models called the Cobra R were produced by SVO's successor, SVT, the Special Vehicle Team. These were delivered without air conditioning, radio, and much of the insulation because the cars were meant for racing purposes. Quite a few, however, ended up racing from stoplight to stoplight.

Ford had done it right for 1994. In the model year, it produced 137,074 cars, ranging in price from the 3.8-liter two-door notchback, at $13,365, up to the non-pace-car Cobra convertible, at $23,535 (coupe at $1,110 less). These numbers represented a nearly 20 percent increase over the 1993 production of 114,228. Sales for '94 were 126,849, one-third more than Chevrolet's Camaro and three times Pontiac's Firebird.

To rectify the 1994 laxity which allowed Cobra R models to end up on the streets and to remain in the good graces of the governmental emission and safety compliance police, the entire run of 250 Cobra R models for 1995 required potential buyers to show valid competition licenses as well as copies of their racing resumes. Priced at $35,499, the R did offer benefits for those who qualified. Produced on the Dearborn assembly line (except for its racing fuel cell and a special engine cooling package), it was a no-frills package: hand-cranked windows, no insulation, radio, or back seat. Seats were minimal trim level because, naturally, racers installed their own competition buckets within their own roll cages. Delivery weight was 3,325 pounds. It was available in any color so long as it was crystal white.

The most exciting news for racers was that Jack Roush Technologies had developed the engine, a 351 Windsor V-8, capable of 300 horsepower at 4,800rpm for these Rs. Roush replaced the Borg-Warner five-speed with a Tremec five-gear box. Final drive was 3.27:1. Suspension was revised, directed by Cobra R Chief Engineer Steve Anderson, and Koni

adjustable shocks reappeared on Mustangs. Tires were special compound P255/45ZR-17 BFGoodrich Comp T/As that appeared shrink-wrapped around 17x9.0-inch alloy wheels.

In November 1994, *Automobile* magazine hinted that the Fox-4 would remain in production, to be replaced before 2004, however, in time for the fortieth anniversary of the Mustang. Rumors emerged and submerged regarding the adaptability of the 4.6-liter Modular V-8, and figures simmered near the surface to hint that the

1995 Cobra R horsepower rating may be what buyers can expect even before the year 2000.

In 1897, Samuel Langhorne Clemens, better known to the world as Mark Twain, cabled from London to the Associated Press in New York. He wrote, "The reports of my death are greatly exaggerated." He lived ten years into the next century, dying in 1910 at 75 years of age.

Throughout American history since October 1962, reports of the death of the T-5, the V-8, and the worldly Fox had been reported and feared. But influences within and without Ford have brought the car back from the dead again and again. In doing so, Ford's stylists from Dave Ash to Bud Magaldi and engineers from Roy Lunn to 1994 Mustang

Power rack-and-pinion steering had a constant ratio of 14.7:1. The Cobra and standard production Mustangs could be ordered with leather surfaces on the articulated sports seats. An AM/FM stereo cassette sound system could be supplemented by the Mach 460 system with a compact disc player. The Cobra interior was available only in black or saddle.

Engineering Manager Kurt Achenbach have established a set of traditions and customs that define Mustang and that keep it alive: It will be a convertible, it will have a V-8, it will be a coupe, it will have an economy engine, it will scorch the pavement and melt its rear tires, it will squeeze a gallon of gas to meet the expectations of those on a budget and a national government on a mission. It will drive by its rear tires, it will sell to young women and to old men. It will accelerate the pulse of every buyer, no matter what age or sex, and it will run and run and run. These goals have become the expectations upon which each new Mustang is founded. After more than thirty years, they are the usual practice, the tradition on which Ford's pony car is reinvented.

In 1934, the English poet T.S. Eliot wrote about tradition. He could have written this as easily for any modern auto enthusiast's magazine any time since April 17, 1964.

"Tradition by itself is not enough; it must be perpetually criticized and brought up to date . . ."

Top
Front suspension was a modified MacPherson Strut-type system with coil springs and a 25-millimeter anti-roll bar. At rear, a four-bar link system reacted with vertical shock absorbers and coil springs and horizontal axle dampers. A 27-millimeter anti-roll bar was fitted as well. Power vented disc brakes were used front and rear, with 13.0-inch-diameter rotors in front, 11.65-inch rotors in back.

Opposite
The Cobra was offered in Crystal White, black clearcoat, and Rio Red tinted clearcoat exterior colors. Riding on Goodyear Eagle GS-C P225/45 ZR17 radial tires, the Cobra was good for 6.3 seconds from 0 to 60 miles per hour and a top speed of around 140 miles per hour. It sold fully equipped for $24,020.

Index